YOU'LL NEVER CHANGE

You'll Never Change.

**CREATE YOUR COMEBACK
& PROVE THEM WRONG**

NATE DUKES

WHAT PEOPLE ARE SAYING ABOUT
YOU'LL NEVER CHANGE...

"This book capture's the attention of people who not only desire change but are committed to it. It provides support, guidance, and hope that you are not alone in an environment that is often scary. Change is one of the only constant things in life. Embrace your change with the help of this amazing book!"

[Cansas Evans]

"I can't say enough about this book. I read almost every page with tears in my eyes because it helped me realize I wasn't alone. The comeback challenges at the end of each chapter are so helpful. I hope whoever reads this book gets what I got out of it. You can change and can do all things with God on your side."

[Craig Hunt]

"This book offered great insight based on real life experiences. Willingness, patience, change, commitment, accountability and integrity are some of the traits described in each chapter. It challenged me to be a better person and do the things I love in life."

[Ron Hinderliter]

"*You'll Never Change* has left me feeling full. Full of hope, love and encouragement! I love the way Nate was vulnerable with his past and was able to articulate his journey without holding back any details. The transformation that took place in Nate's life would make for a great book. However, he took it much further by providing practical action steps and concrete ways to *create your comeback.*"

[Dan Hanna]

"The instructions in this book will change your life if you dare to follow them. This is one I'll refer back to, many times. Having been in recovery for some time, the concept of overcoming addiction is very familiar to me— this is so much more than that— living by your own dreams and designs. Great read, and great book for a big comeback, no matter where you're at in life."

[Ross Thompson]

"*You'll Never Change* was eye opening because it helped me look at my life, my struggles, and what I'm currently going through, and gave me hope in my situation. I can relate to a lot of the hopeless and despairing feelings that Nate felt. It has been very inspiring to see how his struggle has made him stronger and has created a positive mind set. I strongly encourage anyone reading this to participate in the challenges at the end of each chapter!"

[Kevin Koppel]

YOU'LL NEVER CHANGE

ISBN 978-0-578-88996-2
First Edition 2021

Design: Lydia Tarleton

Printed in the United States of America 2021

Request Nate to Speak.

To anyone who thinks their life is too
messed up to change, I wrote this for you.

Contents.

Intro.

(EVERYONE SKIPS THIS, BUT YOU SHOULDN'T)

I know what you're thinking: *is this going to work?* I actually asked myself the same question when I started making my comeback several years ago. My life was stuck in a never ending circle of disappointment in myself because I believed the lie I had been told. ***You'll never change***. Since you're reading this, my guess is you believe that lie too.

Before we go any further I need you to know something — **I believe in you**. I think you're more than a conqueror and everything you need to change is already inside of you. But it doesn't really matter what I think, does it? It matters what you think. There's a good chance you don't think much of yourself right now and you've probably given yourself a good reason to feel that way. Don't worry, I promise to show you how to change that.

But back to the question, *is this going to work?* For some of you... probably not. Now hold on, before you give up, let me explain. Like anything else, your comeback is going to require real work and *a lot* of it. Cliche much? But I'm serious. This book is meant to be a guide that gives you the strategies and motivation you'll need to change your life, but the reality is **you're still in control**. Which means there's a chance you could blow it. Again.

Some of us aren't ready to accept that we're in control of our own decisions and instead we're still looking for someone to come save us. I hate to break it to you but **no one is coming to fix your life for you**.

The good news is that some of you will put in the work and apply what you read in the next chapters. You'll start making your comeback almost immediately, shocking your friends and family who first doubted you. It's a good feeling to confidently walk into a family function without feeling shame.

Let me be clear. The purpose of this book isn't to teach you the fundamentals of overcoming addiction. There's plenty of 12-step programs that can do that. Getting off drugs was one of the hardest things I've ever done. But it wasn't the goal of my life, it was the side effect of wanting more. This book is meant to teach you how to create the life you've always wanted.

You may have given up on things in the past, but I want to encourage you not to give up on yourself this time. I need you to hold on tight because this is just the beginning. *You're about to start from the bottom, create your comeback, and prove them wrong.*

One.

YOU'LL NEVER CHANGE

"STARTED FROM THE BOTTOM NOW WE'RE HERE"
[DRAKE]

I woke up in a panic, completely disoriented and sweating profusely. While my brain was trying to comprehend what was happening, my eyes caught a glimpse of the car dashboard clock.

Nine in the morning is way too early for this right now, my mind said before it was interrupted by the car door being yanked wide opened.

The hands of a stranger reached in, grabbed my shirt, and threw me onto the ground. I looked up to see a police officer with a very unfriendly expression on his face. My brain finally caught up to what was happening, and I knew I was in trouble.

"What's your name?!"
"Where'd you get this car?!"
"Where are the drugs?!"

It became obvious that this officer had no respect for personal space. He was in my face, not asking, but rather yelling question after question at me. And I, of course, had no good answers for any of them. I was not only intimidated by him but also terrified that any answer I gave might incriminate me.

It was the lowest moment I had ever experienced. I was handcuffed, escorted to the back of the cop car, and told to get inside. For the first time ever, I had officially been arrested.

At this point, I'm sure you're probably wondering what led to all of this drama. Let's rewind a little bit so I can provide some context.

Three days earlier, I had stolen a car. Sounds pretty intense — but the truth was, the owner left the keys inside with the door unlocked. I never viewed myself as a thief. But when you find yourself at the wrong place in the wrong headspace, you never know what could happen.

When you find yourself at the wrong place in the wrong headspace, you never know what could happen.

I was desperate. Desperate enough to make me stupid. I never processed that I was taking someone's only way to get to work and make a living for their family. I also never considered the possibility of going to jail. As I held the keys to somebody else's car in my hands, I actually viewed them as a gift. They weren't just the keys to a new vehicle, but also to a new future. To me, they represented a fresh start.

Now obviously, that way of thinking made no sense whatsoever. But my thoughts were compromised by the downward spiral my life was in. And the unhealthy amount of drugs in my system didn't help either. So I stuck the key in the ignition and drove away.

I called one of my buddies who lived in Houston and told him that my life had fallen apart. Of course, I didn't fill him in that I was the reason my life was falling apart. I also didn't tell him I had stolen a car. Instead, I decided to play the best card I had, the one of the victim.

My friend, being the decent human that he was, encouraged me to leave Ohio and come to Houston. He offered a place to stay and help finding a job. I began to think that things were really falling into place! I stopped home, gathered my stuff (a few garbage bags of clothes), and started the long drive to Texas.

I made it all the way to the outskirts of Nashville, Tennessee, before I needed a break. At this point, I had been up for several days straight. My superpowers were stored in my prescription drug cocktail which consisted of Adderall, Xanax, and whatever painkillers I could get my hands on. But as the pills wore off, I started to grow increasingly tired. I knew I needed to pull over and get some rest. I figured it was better to not show up at my friend's house looking like a zombie. Weird that I cared more about that, and not that I'd be arriving in a stolen car.

I pulled into the parking lot of a run-down laundromat, found a spot to park, and closed my eyes. The next thing I knew, I woke up to banging on the car window and yelling. As I sat handcuffed in the cop car, I watched the police search the stolen vehicle. I knew it wouldn't be long before they found my driver's license, ran the vehicle's registration, and confirmed that I was now an official felon.

Every mistake, wrong choice, and inconsiderate decision I had ever made all seemed to catch up to me at once. There would be no Houston, no new job, and no fresh start. Reality settled on my shoulders like a ten thousand pound weight. I had disappointed everyone who had ever loved me, screwed over anybody who had ever trusted me, and blew every chance I was ever given.

I wanted to die. I didn't know how, or when, but if I had an opportunity to kill myself, I probably would have taken it.

How did I get to such a low place in life, where the only solution seemed to be ending everything? The answer seems obvious. I was a screwup, addict, and now a felon. But it wasn't those things, specifically, that left me with an indescribable feeling of hopelessness. Instead, it was a thought that kept replaying over and over again in my mind.

It was the one that simply said, you'll never change.

You Can Change.

I bet you've probably had that same thought, or at least a version of it, at one point or another.

You'll never change.
Things will never get better.
Your life will always suck.

It's effortless to believe the nagging, discouraging voice inside of your head. It's even easier to believe when real voices, from real people, affirm the voice in your head by repeating it to your face. By the way, if you have friends who do that, let me be the first to tell you that you need some new friends. Let me also tell you that, whether it's the voice of someone else or your own, they're lying to you—you can change!

How do I know? Because I did. I'm not in the same physical, mental, emotional, or spiritual place that I was when I sat in the back of that cop car. And if someone would have told me what my future was going to look like back then, I would have laughed in their face! But just because it didn't feel like it could happen, doesn't mean that it didn't.

We will dive further into my life throughout this book, but here are some of my current highlights:

I'm 100% drug free.

I went from stealing cars to owning a car. I know, I know, owning a car isn't really that big of a deal. But when you go to jail for stealing a clunker and driving it across the country, it somehow seems like a big deal to own one yourself! And not only do I own a car, but my wife owns one too, and we just bought our first investment property together last year. Which leads me to my second life highlight.

I have a wife! And Jenna's not just any old wife; she's an amazing person. She was raised with morals and values that led her to give her life to serve and help others. It blows my mind that someone so great would trust me with the responsibility of being her husband. She saw more inside of me than I ever saw in myself, and I couldn't picture having anyone else by my side.

I also have the responsibility, and honor, to work at a church in my hometown. Yes, they really let me work at a real church! (Shoutout to Rust City) Something I also get to do is travel to different locations and speak on stages, to rooms full of people, who are in similar situations that I was several years ago.

I've spent a good portion of my life manipulating, hurting, and taking advantage of other people. Now I get to love, encourage, and push people towards a new possible.

I'm sharing the highlights of my life with you so you can grab ahold of some hope for your life. I don't know what discouraging voices you've been listening to, and believing, lately. But please allow my voice to tell you something different! Here's the truth:

You can change.
Things will get better.
Your life won't always suck.

How do I know? Because everything changed for me. And if it changed for me, it can for you!

Change Requires Commitment.

Change isn't magic. Nobody can wave a wand, make a wish, or will it into existence. You don't go to bed thinking of change and then wake up in the morning completely different. (Wouldn't that be awesome?) The hard truth is this: If you're really going to change, it requires commitment. And while most people want change, very few are willing to commit to the work it takes.

That may be discouraging for some, but I believe it's also very encouraging for others. Commitment is indeed challenging. It requires patience, effort, sacrifice, and all the things we don't naturally like. However, commitment isn't complicated. It doesn't require talent, skill, a big personality, or even for you to fall within a certain tax bracket. The only thing it requires is willingness.

For the rest of this book, we're going to journey through my comeback story together. My promise to you is that I'm going to be as vulnerable as humanly possible. You're going to hear about the good, but also the really bad. Because before every celebration in my life, there was also an intense struggle. It's when we're completely honest about where we've been that we can help others get to where they're going. And I so desperately want you to experience the incredible places you have the potential to go.

I hope my story inspires you, but furthermore, I hope it changes you. For that to happen, we have to discuss what I learned along the way. My comeback didn't just happen; it was the product of committing to the hard work that change requires.

I want you to get the most out of this book, so excuse me for being overly clear about the correct way to use it. Every chapter includes three things:

1. A part of my comeback story (the good, the bad, and the ugly).
2. The lesson I learned from it.
3. A "comeback challenge" to help you take a step toward change.

This book isn't for people who want to hear a nice story, but rather for people who need a comeback. And if you have a willingness to commit to taking the steps this book lays out, your story might just become a book somebody else reads one day! At the very least, you'll be able to live a life you're proud of and can help others do the same.

I don't know what area of your life you need a comeback in. Maybe you're addicted, anxious, ashamed, defeated, depressed, insecure, lazy, or have done some pretty terrible things. What I do know, though, is that your comeback is possible. It's going to be hard work, but this book will guide you every step of the way in creating the comeback you deserve.

Let's dive in and prove every voice that said, *you'll never change*, wrong!

Comeback Challenge.

As I said, every chapter will have a *comeback challenge*. When applied, these challenges will lead you to the change you so desperately desire. And this chapter is no different. Here's your challenge: **Commit to reading this book from front to back.**

We often don't try to change because we're intimidated by the number of areas in our lives that need to change. Please don't feel the pressure that you need to change everything all at once.

The commitment it takes to change one thing is the same commitment you'll need to change everything!

For some of us, it's been a long time since we've followed through on a commitment. But that can change now! It might seem insignificant to finish reading a book. But it's not until you accomplish something small that you can accomplish something big. Today, it's committing to a book! But in the future, it may be committing to a spouse, family, financial investment, dream job, or life of sobriety.

You can't change everything today, but you can commit to begin.

Bonus Challenge.

Don't read this book alone. If you feel stuck right now there's a good chance you have a friend who's feeling the same way and needs to read this, too. Here's some ways you can read this with someone:

1. When you're done reading this book let someone borrow it
2. Invite someone to get the first couple chapters for free at **youllneverchange.com/free**
3. You can gift someone a copy for their birthday just to show them you care.

Having accountability in your life will help you follow through with the commitment you're making. So grab a highlighter (green is my favorite color), mark up this book, and share your journey with someone. I've always gotten more from a book when I had the chance to talk about it with someone else.

Two.

HOW DID I GET HERE?

"I GOT POWER, POISON, PAIN, AND JOY INSIDE MY DNA"
[KENDRICK LAMAR]

My story didn't start in the back of a cop car. Instead, the beginning chapters of my life began at Lancer Court, the government housing I lived in as a kid. Many dysfunctional experiences shaped me into the person I became. A laundry list of poor decisions also guaranteed my downward spiral. But let's start by taking a look at how I grew up.

I love my parents a ton, but the truth is, they were trying to figure a lot of things out when they were young. They tried their best, but they didn't get everything right. And as a kid, it's pretty common to become a product of your environment without realizing it. Why? Because some things are taught, while others are caught. And before I had the mental capacity to recognize it, I caught a lot of broken mindsets from a lot of broken people.

My parents had an "on-again, off-again" relationship. One month we'd be one big happy family, and the next, we wouldn't be living under the same roof. It produced emotional as well as financial instability. We ended up living in Lancer Court because we couldn't make it on our own with the chaos that existed in our lives.

The Government wasn't our only form of assistance. Members from our local church would also donate to our family. Sometimes they gave gifts to us for the holiday's, and other times they gave cash to help keep on the electricity. Whatever it was, it felt like we were always receiving a handout.

I still remember one Christmas in pretty vivid detail. At

that point, my parents had just gotten back together, and they were simply trying to make it work. My mom pulled us aside to let us know there wouldn't be much underneath the tree that year. As a kid, that's never what you want to hear. I'm sure you can relate.

But on Christmas Eve, my mom dropped us off at a friend's house to hang out. When we came back home, there were a massive amount of presents, not just underneath the tree, but all throughout the room. At first, it felt like we hit the jackpot! We thought we were getting nothing, and all of a sudden, we had the same magical Christmas experience as all of our friends. However, having a "normal" Christmas didn't make us a "normal" family.

While I was grateful for the gifts, I also had an awareness that they didn't come from my parents. Someone took my mom shopping so she could give us the Christmas we deserved. I became accustomed to depending on handouts, hand-me-downs, and other people.

Living this way developed a couple of unhealthy mentalities on the inside of me. Maybe you can relate:

1. There must be something wrong with me.

I remember looking at what everybody else had, and it always seemed like they had more than we did. Comparison will quickly steal your contentment. And mine was taken from me at a young age. I felt less valuable than the kids who didn't have to buy their clothes from Goodwill. Even though I appreciated my mom calling it "Gucci's" to try to make it seem like we were wearing the best of the best. It was more likely for me to ride a bike from someone's trash rather than one bought from a store. It seemed like the kids who had the nicest stuff were the most happy. Therefore, I believed the lie that I'd never be happy because to me happiness = things.

*Disclaimer: I don't think there's anything wrong with getting things second hand. I still like to shop at "Gucci's".

2. My situation will never change

I didn't realize it then, but I was definitely taught how to navigate life with a poverty mindset. I believed there wasn't enough money to go around for everybody. And we probably wouldn't be the ones to get what was available! By default, I thought that I had to be stuck in the same situation for the rest of my life. I didn't understand that you could dream, plan, and work your way into a different reality. But you don't know, what you don't know.

The truth is, we all grow up with unhealthy mentalities. I genuinely believe that most parents, grandparents, and role models do the best they can. But imperfect people always pass on imperfect qualities to those they raise up. And the mindsets we inherit during childhood travel with us into adulthood.

Maybe you're currently living with the same unhealthy mentalities I was. Or perhaps yours are slightly different. Regardless of what they are, I want to make sure you know that you can relearn another way of thinking. But relearning takes unlearning. We have to acknowledge that our current way of thinking, which feels natural to us now, isn't the right way of thinking. Once we recognize that our thought patterns are unhealthy, we can stop shaping our actions around them. And start making better choices.

My unhealthy mentalities led me to make decisions that landed me in a jail cell. Thankfully I no longer live guided by the same way of thinking today. It wasn't too late for me, and it's not too late for you!

Today vs. Tomorrow.

There's one lesson that has changed a lot for me. If you don't learn this, you won't make much progress in creating your comeback story and transforming into the person you'd like to be: Don't play for today, play for tomorrow.

Growing up, I never knew you could have a vision for your life that's greater than your "right now." It's challenging to think about tomorrow when you're so focused on how to get through today. Sure, our family had a desire for a different future, but those wishes eventually became suppressed. Why? The chaos of our today required all of our attention.

Any mentality that says "you'll never change" gets you stuck in what I call a hamster wheel.

Think about the unfortunate reality of a pet hamster for a second. They live their life inside of a glass cage. They get to spend their day looking at freedom but have no way to get there. One of the only things they have to do is run on their wheel. And while it does burn a lot of energy, it's probably a pretty depressing reminder that as hard as they try, they'll never actually go anywhere.

As hard as I try, I'll never actually go anywhere.

I believed that lie. A lot of you believe that lie right now. And if you accept it as truth, eventually you'll stop trying to go anywhere.

When you only focus on today instead of tomorrow, you don't believe you can ever change. Your environment becomes your identity. You stop looking outside the glass, dreaming about the freedom you could have in the future, and just keep running on the wheel. Eventually, tomorrow is no longer something you even think about as you become trapped by today.

If you ever want to change, you can't lose vision for tomorrow. It will seem impossible, but you can't allow your mind to lose the picture of what you want your life to look like. Because as soon as it does, you get stuck. You end up going around and around on the same wheel. It's possible to run really fast in life but go nowhere that matters. A vision for tomorrow is the thing that gets you off the wheel.

It's possible to run really fast in life but go nowhere that matters.

Doing and Dreaming.

What is vision? Merriam-Webster defines it like this: *A manifestation of something immaterial.*[1]

I love that definition. Having vision for your life starts as something immaterial. It's simply the best, most noble, honorable, and unique thing you can think up. But what starts as immaterial has the ability to become reality.

Every present reality is someone's past vision. It's not until something is thought about that it can be planned for. And it's not until a plan is developed that it can be pursued.

So if we're going to be people who play for tomorrow, vision is important. But how do you develop a vision for your life? Here are a few tips:

1. Do Stuff!

We've been created with unique talents, gifts, interests, passions, and things that make our hearts come alive. The only way to discover what you love and what you're good at, is by trying new things. You didn't know you liked macaroni and cheese until you tasted it. But once those cheesy carbs hit your belly, it felt like heaven. In the same way, it's through the process of trying things in life that you find what you really want to do. As cliche' as sounds, don't be afraid to try something else.

2. Dream BIG

"The greatest danger for most of us is not that our aim is too high and we miss it, but that it is too low and we reach it." -Michelangelo

What could your future look like? The temptation is to

scale your dreams according to the size of your current reality. But if you don't shoot for big, you'll never go far. Don't be afraid to be outlandish, wild, and crazy with it.

While sitting in a jail cell I never thought I'd write a book let alone have someone reading it.

The truth is, our lives don't end up looking exactly like we envisioned. But Dreams are what give us direction. And at the very least, it's better to be moving in the right direction than not moving at all.

Most of the time, when you ask people what they want their lives to look like, they have no idea. And that breaks my heart. It's unfortunate because it doesn't have to be that way. Dreams aren't just for the rich, privileged, educated, or those who have always gotten it right. They're for people like us, trying to fix our life and make a comeback.

Five minutes of dreaming today might lead to the comeback you'll have five years from now!

Comeback Challenge.

I know it's probably been awhile since some of you have considered what your tomorrow can look like. The dreams in your heart have probably been dormant for a long time. And whenever you start to stir those things up, it's natural to become fearful and doubtful. But emotions like fear and doubt are actually indicators that you're headed in the right direction. They prove the significance of your vision.

So even if you feel afraid right now, or think this whole dreaming thing is dumb, let me push you one step further and give you some inspiration. Here's your "comeback challenge" for chapter 2: **Create a vision for your life.**

What could 5 years from now look like for you? Take a second, an hour, or a day to write out your vision for your life.

Maybe your vision Is that your family is stable, your finances are finally secure, you don't depend on drugs to get through the day, maybe you want to start a business. Whatever your vision looks like write it down, and allow yourself to dream.

It's easy to write something and forget it, so the second part of this challenge is to remind yourself of your vision daily. Set a reminder on your phone, right now, to read your vision every day. I'm serious. Put the book down and set a reminder, your future self will thank you.

Bonus Challenge.

I know it's hard to imagine your life looking any different than what it does right now. But I remember being exactly where you're at and writing a vision for what my life could look like. If you'd like to see the vision I wrote for my future, my family, and even this book you can download and read it at **youllneverchange.com/vision.**

I hope as you read what I wrote, it inspires you to write your own and to dream big.

Three.

WHAT IS WRONG WITH ME?

"I'VE GOT SOME ISSUES THAT NOBODY CAN SEE"
[KID CUDI]

As the end of high school approached, I knew I wanted a better life than the one I had growing up. But to make more money, create stability, and become a baller, I thought I needed education. After getting rejected by The Ohio State University I applied to the University of Akron, which was about an hour away from home. It was close enough to drive back whenever I needed, and far enough to create some separation from family. That distance proved to be dangerous.

I have to be honest; college was dual-purposed. There was definitely a part of me which was motivated to better myself. But there was another part of me that just wanted to escape. I just wanted to get away from the chaos of my childhood. I didn't like the hand I was dealt as a kid and hoped that my cards would change by going to college. I wanted to be someone different, or at the very least feel something different. Have you ever been there?

It was during my freshman year that I was introduced to drugs and alcohol. Chances are, you probably know how it works. There are moments of exposure to substances in high school, but if you're lucky, it's sporadic and doesn't really affect your life all that much. However, when you go to a public university, the exposure becomes much more consistent. Drugs used to be hard and scary to get your hands on, but now they're everywhere and easy to get. And when you're looking for an escape, exposure inevitably leads to experimentation.

Like most, it started with drinking alcohol consistently. I understand that alcohol is pretty standard in our culture, and some can drink without abuse. However, I was underage and drinking to drown out all the things I didn't like about myself. And even though I didn't realize what I was doing in the moment, looking back, I can see the danger. I liked the feeling it gave me. And after feeling bad for eighteen years, you'll maximize whatever makes you feel good.

When it comes to substances, typically, one serves as a gateway to another. And the more I drank, the more comfortable I was with being under the influence. I went to college for four years. It's the same amount of time that most take to graduate, but I managed to come nowhere near a degree. Honestly, I don't remember much about what I studied. But I do remember the drugs I took.

The first drug I got into was marijuana (weed, pot, whatever you call it. It's all the same)

One of my college roommates was your stereotypical college stoner, always smoking weed. Every night, I'd hear him laughing in his room with a few of his buddies. As I listened to them giggle like little girls night after night, I started to grow more and more curious. He seemed to be having way more fun than me. Eventually, my curiosity led me to accept their offer to join.

They taught me how to use a bong while I sat on their bunk beds. We passed it back and forth as my eyes glossed over and my stomach craved Taco Bell. I promised you that I'd be honest at the beginning of this book. So in the spirit of transparency, it was a very fun night! I've never laughed so long and hard about well… nothing. However, sometimes what feels fun in the moment isn't actually good for your future.

But I wasn't living for the future; I was living for the now. I wanted to feel nothing or to feel something. I just desired to escape. So one thing led to another, and before I knew it, I was no longer just smoking weed, but popping pills that were just as easy to get. It was only a matter of time right?

Sometimes what feels fun in the moment isn't actually good for your future.

The more I partied, the less I studied. Which was a problem because I needed to keep my grades high enough to stay in school. During my sophomore year, I had a huge test I needed to study for. I had only been to class a few times that semester, so I didn't know any of the content. My only hope was to pull an all-nighter studying the notes a classmate had taken.

While I was venting about my self-inflicted stress to a friend, he offered me something called Adderall. I didn't fully understand what it was at the time. I just knew it was an orange pill that people took to help them study. It seemed harmless and also helpful!

Time for another honest moment. As soon as it got into my system, I felt unstoppable. If you don't know what Adderall is, it's a prescription drug for those diagnosed with ADHD. After taking it I was able to study without sleep the entire night before the test. I had a laser-like focus that I'd never experienced before. And surprisingly, I got a pretty good grade.

It really only took once to get me hooked. I was focused, energized, and more confident! And I never wanted to go without the superpowers it seemed to provide again. At one point I remember "thanking God" for sending this into my life.

As I started to "feel myself" more and more, I gained increased confidence in trying harder drugs. I said yes to cocaine at a party without even thinking twice. It seemed as if my conscience wasn't considering right and wrong, or good and bad, anymore. My appetite for a high was larger than the one I had for the law, morals, or my future.

Obviously, this eventually led to significant problems in my life. Looking back, if I hadn't become so hooked on substances, I probably wouldn't have stolen that car. A lifestyle of addiction eventually causes a lot of pain, chaos, and destruction. Not just for you, but also for those around you. And when you're not in your right mind, you start to think one lousy decision might un-do all the other wrong decisions you've made throughout the years. You might even believe your fresh start lies within driving a car that isn't yours across the country.

In retrospect, it wasn't those first nights of trying drugs that were the problem. But the next night, and the next night, and the nights after that. And pretty soon, every day, you're chasing the same high you initially felt. But it only leaves you empty. So you consume drink after drink, pill after pill, or hit after hit, hoping this time will be the time you become more whole. But in my pursuit of wholeness, my emptiness grew deeper.

The weed intended to help me feel nothing became what I needed to feel anything.

The Adderall I used to help me study became what I thought I needed to survive.

The cocaine and pain killers I tried led me to living a life dependent on Xanax and being okay with it.

Substances were no longer something I wanted, but something I needed. I couldn't go without them. Which is the definition of addiction.

Let's get real for a second. You don't have to pop a pill or snort a powder to be an addict. We all have unhealthy dependencies that we use to escape. How do you determine if you have an addiction? It's simple; pay attention to your appetite. An uncontrollable appetite, always reveals where your addiction lies.

All addiction is detrimental. The truth is, an addiction to sex is just as dangerous as one to a substance. The craving for achievement can be just as intense as the one for Adderall. The desire for likes on social media can lead you to lose sight of what's actually important in life. The need to prove yourself can damage you just as much as popping a pill.

We all do things for different reasons. For me, I wasn't happy with myself. I didn't enjoy being the chubby kid who couldn't get girls. I felt like my life circumstances put me at a disadvantage. I didn't even like, much less love, who I was. And that self-hatred drove every poor decision I ever made in college.

What's driving you? It could be several things. Maybe it's self-hatred, insecurity, fear, greed, lack of community, your parents not loving you, or a coach saying you weren't good enough. We're all driven by different motivations. But regardless of what your motivations are, here's what I know.

What drives us influences the decisions we make, both

good and bad. And our lives become a product of what we repeatedly decide to do.

The Power of a Decision.

My favorite personal development author is Tony Robbins. I once listened to his teaching on the power of decisions, and it has always stuck with me. His quote below sums up the main idea of it pretty well.

"At any moment, the decisions you make can change the course of your life forever."

What he's saying is that your life is shaped by the decisions you've made up to this point. I want you to take a moment right now and think about your life. Think about how differently it could have looked if you would had made one or two different decisions. Good or bad it doesn't matter. I don't want you to buy into the idea that you should have known the right answers, but I do want you to see the power of your decisions.

Let me explain.

Have you ever made the decision to move to a new area at some point in your life. Did you find love? Find a best friend? Get a new job? If so, your decision to move affected the outcome of your life, maybe without you even realizing it.

Whether you make decisions that are good, bad, or a combination of both, you can't deny the power your decisions have!

When I look back on those four years of college, I did learn one huge lesson: Decisions determine destiny.

The decision I made to try weed on my roommate's bunk bed proved to be one that would change the course of my life forever. But at the moment, it didn't feel like it. That's how powerful decisions can be.

We think it's the big decisions that define us, but it's often the small ones that change our direction.

In the same way, even if your life is a complete mess right now, you're only one or two decisions away from a new destiny. I hope that encourages you! While new decisions might be hard to make, they're yours to make. Will new decisions bring you outside of your comfort zone and challenge how you've grown accustomed to living? Most likely! But difficult doesn't mean impossible. And if you want a new life, you have the power to make some new decisions.

Life Conditions vs. Life Decisions.

Hopefully, by this point in the chapter, you're at least considering making some new decisions. You may still be contemplating if you have the grit inside of you to put your foot down and make them. I feel it's important to warn you about something you'll probably run into. Your life's condition is going to say you can't make a new life decision.

That's a lie, of course. But just because it isn't true doesn't mean your life's condition won't be a challenge to overcome.

We all have different conditions in life. Sometimes conditions are created, and other times they're out of your control. What are some conditions that stand in opposition to you making better decisions?

- Maybe you were born into a broken home, and your parents weren't there the way they should have been.
- Maybe you can't afford the education you deserve.
- Maybe you aren't as talented as a friend of yours.
- Maybe your spouse doesn't support your dreams the way they should.
- Maybe your coach isn't giving you an opportunity to shine.
- Maybe you've been battling addiction for as long as you can remember.
- Maybe fear and anxiety have robbed your ability to dream.

I don't know your current condition, but I know your decisions don't have to be affected by it! If you buy the lie then you really won't change and your comeback will stay on pause.

Comeback Challenge.

The "comeback challenge" for this chapter is an extension from chapter 2 where I encouraged you to dream and create a vision for the future you. I hope you took some time to do that, and if you haven't, it's still not too late. Here's your challenge: **Stay in the mindset of the futuristic you. You've crushed your comeback and proved everyone who ever said, "you'll never change," wrong. What decisions would you have to make today in order to experience that future?**

- Maybe you need to call a rehab center.
- Maybe you need to sign up for counseling.
- Maybe you need to apply for college or a new job.
- Maybe you need to set aside time for your growth.
- Maybe you need to start serving others through a local church or non-profit.

I don't know what the decisions are, but I do know your destiny lies within them!

Bonus Challenge.

Changing your life isn't easy, so I created a 30 day challenge that's focused on helping you make new decisions. If you'd like to take the challenge or hear from those who've already done it, go to **youllneverchange.com/challenge.**

Four.

HOW DO I MAKE MORE MONEY?

"MO MONEY, MO PROBLEMS"
[THE NOTORIOUS B.I.G]

I went to college for four years and managed to not graduate. When most of my friends were getting degrees, I had to face the sad reality that my education was going nowhere. So like the other broke college students who served their time before me, I returned home to live with my parents, again. Talk about a walk of shame.

Once I got home, I was determined not to work a regular job. There's nothing wrong with that, but at that moment, I was convinced there was. I didn't want to live the same life my parents had. I wanted more money, stuff, and an impressive social status. I didn't have a degree but was filled with motivation and grit. I had no idea I was actually driven by trying to avoid embarrassment. But it drove me all the way to starting my own marketing agency.

I know you've heard some of the same inspiring stories as me. You know, the ones where people fail out of college, start their own businesses, and become wildly successful. Let me be clear. That is not my story... which, strangely, should be reassuring for you. After all, this book isn't for people who've gotten everything right. Instead, it's for those fighting for a comeback.

Anyways, I had a *little bit* of success. And when I say a little bit, I mean a tiny bit! I stayed afloat for about a year, but the truth was, I had no education in marketing. I also had very little guidance. I was on an island all by myself, just trying to figure it out. All the while, my primary source of fuel was still my prescription drug cocktail. Add all of that together, and it definitely wasn't a formula for long term career sustainability.

A buddy of mine approached me about joining him on

a new venture. He knew I had started a business and therefore had an entrepreneurial spirit. He wanted to open a new bar in Youngstown, Ohio. One conversation led to another and after several meetings I became a part owner and investor.

My job was to focus on building the business. And focus I did. Actually, I was so focused that I became obsessive. There was a three-month period where I even slept at the bar. It wasn't because I financially needed to. But I wanted to put every ounce of energy I had into making it succeed. I didn't even want to waste the time it took to drive there in the morning!

And honestly, the hard work paid off. Over a short period of time, we built something that was considered to be successful. (at least in my eyes it was) But the way we got to success wasn't the healthiest. There wasn't very much sleep or self-care involved, but lots of Adderall instead. I figured it was the sacrifice you had to make to win. And winning was the only thing I cared about. #winning

There were some perks to success. I had access to money like I had never seen before. That's not saying it was very much, but since I grew up with so little, it was more than I knew what to do with. I had a beautiful apartment within walking distance of the bar, right in downtown. For the first time ever, it was easy to get girls. The people in my life viewed me as accomplished. And it was nice to prove everybody who underestimated me wrong after I had completely failed at college.

I got everything I thought I had ever wanted. And I was absolutely *miserable.*

It was a pretty shocking reality for a kid who didn't grow up with much. We tend to believe that happiness lies within what we don't have. We think that if we could just be more successful than we currently are, then everything in life will fall into place. Happiness, contentment, and inner-peace must follow. That idea is one of the most commonly accepted deceptions of our current culture and I found that out the hard way. It's possible to be successful and miserable at the same time.

I hope to teach you from the pain I experienced.

Success vs. Fulfillment.

You may have heard it said before that "what you look for is what you'll find." I think that statement is more than a cliché and holds up to be true throughout life. Whatever you put intentional focus into over a long period of time will ultimately produce results.

For me, I put all of my focus on succeeding at the bar. You know the saying, "you have to eat, sleep, and drink it?" Well, I literally ate, slept, and drank there. It wasn't because it was a quality lifestyle, or even made me super happy. If anything, it left me empty. It simply was because I valued success over everything else and was willing to do whatever it took to get it.

That sounds admirable, but the truth is, it really wasn't. The only reason I wanted to succeed was that I was trying to fill voids that existed in my heart. I still hadn't healthily processed the brokenness from my childhood. I thought the way to overcome was to produce a reality that was opposite from it.

Brokenness is an interesting thing, though. You don't magically become unbroken just because everything looks good on the outside. In other words, you can't "succeed" it away. Brokenness travels with you from one season to another, whether you appear to be winning or losing. Why? Because internal problems can't be fixed with external solutions.

The truth is, if you're hyper-focused on success, you're probably going to find it sooner or later. But let me ask you a question. Is success the thing that's actually worth finding?

Success can never fix you, but it will always expose you. A lack of influence with people creates a safer space to process your issues. That's why it's a good idea to deal with what's going on inside of you first. Because as soon as your influence grows, your issues get magnified.

We'll dive further into this in the next chapter, but the bar's success led to the exposure of my internal issues. And they didn't only affect me, but also everyone else around me.

When I was working at growing the bar, I thought it was teaching me all sorts of valuable lessons about business, leadership, and winning. And I suppose it did teach me some principles in that vein. But looking back, there was one lesson way more valuable that I learned. Here's what it is:

Stop focusing on success and start focusing on fulfillment.

Success is a pretty crappy thing to chase when it's the only thing you care about. Don't get me wrong, success isn't a bad thing. I want to succeed at what I'm passionate about! And I hope you find success as well.

But success doesn't lead to fulfillment. I know we want it too. And I know we've been told that it will. But let me be the first to say to you from a place of experience, it doesn't.

As long as there's still emptiness on the inside of you, you'll do whatever it takes to fill it. That's why some people are successful yet still addicted. That's why some rich people work ridiculous overtime to try to get even richer. That's why some people continue to buy bigger houses even though they can't even fill the space they have now.

If we aren't careful, success can lead to excessive striving. The more you get, the more you want. And you can waste your entire life chasing something you're never going to catch. It's not until we are fulfilled that we can truly be at peace with ourselves.

Selfless > Selfish.

So if success doesn't lead to fulfillment, what does?

A group of scientists started a study in 1938 during the Great Depression. They followed 268 Harvard sophomores for nearly eighty years of their lives, hoping to find what led to a life of health and happiness. They eventually expanded the study to include the Harvard students' offspring, which now number around 1,300. And looking to diversify the data even further, the scientists added a group of 456 Boston inner-city residents in the 1970s. While all of them journeyed through the ups and downs of life, they collected countless amounts of data on the state of their physical and mental health.

As you can imagine, some of the participants went on to become wildly successful businessmen, doctors, lawyers. Others ended up as schizophrenics and alcoholics. A quote from the Harvard Gazette perfectly sums up what the results proved to show:

"Close relationships, more than money or fame, are what keep people happy throughout their lives," the study revealed. "Those ties protect people from life's discontents, help to delay mental and physical decline, and are better predictors of long and happy lives than social class, IQ, or even genes. That finding proved true across the board among both the Harvard men and the inner-city participants."[1]

Our fulfillment isn't generated by our success but rather by the people around us! The truth is, our desire for success is typically motivated by selfishness. We want to be successful because we think it'll make us feel good. We want people to look at us and say, "WOW". We take pride in the popularity and possessions that come along with making it big. Selfishness and success sometimes work together. But selfishness and

If we genuinely want to find fulfillment, we must learn to live selflessly rather than selfishly.

fulfillment do not. If we genuinely want to find fulfillment, we must learn to live selflessly rather than selfishly.

Let me talk about something crazy.

Selflessness is less about you and more about other people. What does that look like? It looks like giving your life to add value to others rather than yourself. It's not about you helping you, it's about you helping those around you.

At the church I work at, my job is to lead our serve teams. Literally, all day and every day, I invest in people so that they'll invest in other people. It's hard to explain if you've never experienced it, but something special happens when you choose to serve somebody else. Taking your focus off making your life better and putting it on making someone else's life better leads to true fulfillment. When you help other people with their issues, your issues look a lot smaller.

Selfishness seeks success at all costs. But selflessness seeks out serving at all costs.

Selfishness is hungry for money. But selflessness only cares about bringing meaning to others.

Selfishness is obsessed with looking impressive. Selflessness is too busy helping others to worry about what it looks like.

I can't guarantee that pursuing fulfillment will lead you to a life of looking wildly successful in the world's eyes. But I can guarantee that your life and the world will become better places when you do.

Comeback Challenge.

This challenge is going to seem counterproductive to your comeback, but trust me, it's one of the most important things you can do. I don't want us to get so focused on us helping ourselves get better that we forget about other people. We only become better people when we help make other people better. Here's your challenge: **Pick one thing you can do this week to make somebody's life a little better. Then do it the week after that, the one after that, and every one for the rest of your life!**

The significant thing about being selfless is that it's simple. You don't have to do anything groundbreaking to make somebody's day. It can be as simple as complimenting a stranger, writing a card to a friend, paying for someone's meal, or shoveling your neighbor's driveway.

Whatever it is, start to build the habit of selflessness.

If you do, you'll show the voices which said "you'll never change" that you already are!

Bonus Challenge.

I want to celebrate and share your stories of selflessness. Go to **youllneverchange.com/story**, take a picture, and tell me how you've helped someone this week.

You can also check out **@whoisnatedukes** on Instagram to see other people's stories of selflessness.

Five.
THIS IS THE END

"YOU CAN TELL THEM THAT I'VE BEEN FROM HELL AND BACK"
[KID INK]

After the last chapter, you know that success doesn't equal fulfillment. I became more successful than people ever expected me to be and more miserable than I'd ever been. In the same way that success leaves you empty, so does stuff. Money and possessions fail time and time again to satisfy our souls.

During my time at the bar, I frequently found myself chasing the next high. Since success wasn't cutting it, I figured there had to be something that would help me feel whole. As I strived for new levels of success, I also started gambling.

When you grow up with so little, your sole focus is getting more. Unfortunately, you never actually learn how to manage what you have. You also never plan for what you would do with the money if you actually ever made it. It's a prime example of a lack of vision coming back to bite you in the butt. Your resources can't keep you where vision didn't take you. Lack of planning for the future will eventually catch up.

Even though I learned how to make money, I never developed a new mentality to go with it. I still operated like I was lacking. I wanted more and more. And although greed probably played a part in my motivation, I don't believe it was the primary gasoline source fueling my life.

Gambling temporarily satisfied my competitive nature. My insecurity hated losing more than anything else. Whenever I lost, whether it was at cards or corn hole, I felt like the poor kid that everybody looked at with judgmental eyes. And I know I have some competitive people reading this that will relate to the next statement. It seems silly, but I hated losing even more than I liked winning.

The desire to win at all costs might work on a football field, but it's not good when it comes to casinos. Wanting to win at all costs, will cost more than you're willing to pay.

I won't dive into all of the details of how a casino works. The main ways I liked to gamble were slot machines, table games, and cards.

Regardless of how you choose to gamble, there is one constant. You always have to bet money to make money. And the more you risk, the bigger the potential payout is. This makes competitive people come alive, thinking their drive to win can carry them to victory. However, there's one major problem. Casinos only make money when you lose yours. Therefore, the odds are always set against you. Literally the House always wins.

Let me give you an example.

Even though I won sometimes, I never learned to walk away. Winning made me arrogant. I believed I was smarter than the machines and people I was playing against. I knew countless people before me had lost numerous amounts of money, but I thought I'd be different!

Gambling is like dating the girl who makes you feel good when you hang out but is cheating on you behind your back. She's only concerned with what she can get out of you. So while the relationship gives you the goosebumps temporarily, it will inevitably end in disaster. Not everything that makes you feel good is actually good for your future.

And gambling mixed with drugs was not good for my future. Every time I won a little bit of money, I'd bet it away trying to win more. My appetite was bigger than my bank account. Eventually, I wasted all of the money I won and

Not everything that makes you feel good is actually good for your future.

everything I had in my checking and savings. But even then, I couldn't stop. I sold everything of value I owned so I could continue to return to the casino. I was a drug addict, willing to give up everything for one more bet.

I gambled my way into having nothing. I was completely addicted. And even though my resources ran dry, I couldn't stop. That's when I made one of the worst decisions of my life.

My bank account was empty, but the business' was not. And as part-owner, I had full access to make withdraws. That's when "borrowing" large sums of money from the business account started happening. I say I borrowed it because I had every intention of paying it back. I figured that when I won, I could even pay back a little bit of interest. It would be good for the bar. Good for my business partner. Good for me. Good for my addiction. It would be a win-win for all parties involved.

The problem was that I didn't win. I lost. All of it. And it was only a matter of time before the successful businessman I had become was exposed.

One day my business partner called me into his office and asked if I had handed out the checks for payroll. With sweaty palms and a shaky voice, I broke the news to him that we didn't have enough money in the account to pay anybody.

He was confused. He was panicked. He was frustrated. And finally, his mind caught up to his emotions. He figured out that I had stolen the money and gambled away payroll the night before. He was done with me, and understandably so. He gave me two options, to sign the bar over to him and walk away or lawyers were getting involved. I never stepped foot in the bar I had worked so hard to build again. It's a miracle he didn't press charges against me. And I'm forever grateful to him for that.

Looking back, it's actually unbelievable to me that I ever got to such a low place in life. It's not the fact that I had an addiction or wasted all of my money that was so shocking. It's not even stealing from the bar that throws my mind into a whirl. It's the manner in which I did so.

My decisions didn't just ruin my life, but ruined the lives of those around me. Those paychecks were the way that our twenty employees were able to provide for their families. It's how they put food on the table for their kids. It's the way they paid the rent and kept the lights on.

I ruined my life, career, and one of the best friendships I had. But I also risked ruining the lives of those who trusted me. I put the entire future of the business in jeopardy.

For what? It all started because I lacked gratitude. I wasn't grateful for what I had, even though it was more than I knew what to do with. And I figured if what I had didn't fill me up, then "more" must be the answer. It was in the pursuit of "more" that I lost everything.

Choose Gratitude.

(before you write this off as another gratitude list, hear me out)

I believe one of the most undervalued superpowers in society today is gratitude. I call it a superpower because I really think it allows us to live on a different level. It helps us to see life through a new lens that completely shifts our perspective. And if anything is going to shift our lives (aka change), it starts with a shift in perspective.

My gambling addiction was a product of not being grateful for what I had. But the crazy thing is, I can now see that I had so much to be thankful for. Even though running a bar isn't what I'd give my life to today, some things were really going my way in that context. I had a stable job, a friend who believed in me, money, a car, and a downtown apartment. And past just external things, there were also things with more value and substance. I was healthy, had a purpose, growth opportunities, and the influence to better the lives of those around me.

I had more than what most people could ever hope for. I just didn't realize it at the time. The only thing I could pay attention to was my hunger for more. Here's the greatest lesson I learned in that season: When you're grateful for what you have, you can't be consumed by what you don't have.

What you don't have is definitely a motivator. But it doesn't always motivate you in the right direction. Gratitude

When you're grateful for what you have, you can't be consumed by what you don't have.

keeps your motives pure. When you're thankful for what you have, you don't need more. It allows you to pursue goals without an unhealthy drive attached to them. An unhealthy drive doesn't care how you get something; it only cares that you get it. It can lead to gambling, cutting corners, unnecessary risk, performance identity, and anxieties that stem from obsession.

Gratitude reminds us that regardless of whether we have a little or a lot, we have enough, and we are enough. Should you give up on your dreams and goals? No way! Should you stop working hard at the things you want to unfold in your life? Absolutely not. But when you're grateful, you can do

Gratitude reminds us that regardless of whether we have a little or a lot, we have enough, and we are enough.

things the right way because you're in a healthy place.

Something special happens when your identity isn't rooted in what you do or don't have. Living from a place of wholeness is a beautiful thing to observe.

I know, I know. It sounds good in theory. But here's what you might be thinking: *I don't have anything to be grateful for.*

Listen, I'm not the guy that wants to fill you with fluff and empty encouragement. I understand you might be reading this book during one of the lowest moments of your life. If things were going perfectly, or even well, you probably wouldn't have picked up this book in the first place. I fully understand that some of you may be actively addicted, relationally broken, abandoned by those you love, or flat out broke. But at the risk of offending you, can I propose an idea to you?

This may be the lowest moment of your life, but don't let yourself play the victim. You have something to be grateful for.

You might have a million things to be ungrateful for. But when you have one thing you wake up grateful for every single day, you have something to continue to live for. You have a reason to move forward, work on yourself, and get better.

Don't know what to be grateful for? Maybe you'll resonate with one of the following:

- One person who cares about you.
- A place to live. Even if it's not yours.
- A car to drive. Even if it's crappy.
- Kids who want their parents around more than anything else. Even if they don't say it.
- A job. Even if it's not the one you want.
- An opportunity.
- Someone who gives you good advice. An author who wrote a book about your comeback because he believes in you!

When you think about it, there's always something to be grateful for. And usually, it's pretty significant. But even if you're being stubborn or find yourself in a completely hopeless state of mind, there's still one thing you can be grateful for.

You woke up this morning with a heartbeat. And as long as your heart is beating, there's still hope.

We never had to do anything to earn or deserve the lives we've been allowed to live. The beating of our hearts and breath in our lungs are gifts given to us at birth. And as long as they're still happening, our lives are valuable. Valuable enough to take up space and air on this planet. Valuable enough to contribute. Valuable enough to make a difference. Valuable enough to turn things around.

Somebody cares about you. If you think they don't, you're wrong. And I would know best because I know that I care! God thought highly enough about you to give you the gift of life. If that's all you have, that's all you need! And because He cares, so do I.

Comeback Challenge.

Here's the thing, if you wanted to, you could live a life defined by gratitude. But it only happens intentionally, not accidentally. So here's the challenge I'm going to leave you with this chapter: **Write down at least one thing you're grateful for. Every day. Time to set another reminder in your phone. If you haven't learned by now, I'm serious.**

If you're struggling to think of something, change the challenge. Write down one thing you would be grateful for if you wanted to be grateful. We often aren't grateful simply because we don't want to be or think we can't.

Truthfully, you'll probably be able to think of way more than one. That's the thing about gratitude, it's contagious.

When you realize one thing worth being grateful for, it typically leads to a revelation of many more. Before you know it, you can start to live with an attitude of gratitude.

Gratitude isn't necessarily natural. For some reason, as we become a little bit hardened by life, we tend to prioritize pessimism over optimism. That's why I love the habits one of my buddies applies to his life. Every time he pulls up to a traffic light, he verbalizes something he's grateful for. The more lights he hits, the more appreciation he starts to develop.

Can I encourage you? Being grateful for what you have is more fulfilling than being frustrated with what you don't! Chances are, you're probably closer to your comeback than you think, but it's activated by gratitude.

Bonus Challenge.

Take a picture of your gratitude list, tag me in it using **@whoisnatedukes**, and add the hashtag #youllneverchange.

Six.

WHAT HAPPENS IF I RUN AWAY?

"BRAND NEW WHIP
JUST HOPPED IN"
[JACK HARLOW]

When I signed over the bar, walked away from my most significant accomplishment, and lost my income. I obviously could no longer afford the lifestyle I had grown so accustomed to. That included my downtown apartment, car, and any remaining possession that wasn't sold for gambling money. I had nothing. No where to live no way to get around. It was time for part 2 of moving back in with mom and dad.

I'm very thankful my parents allowed me to sleep on their couch and interrupt their lives. While our family was not perfect, they really did care about me. They always wanted what was best for my life. Looking back, I'm sure I put them through hell during this season. No parent wants to watch their kid struggle while unwilling to accept any help. They didn't know the depths of everything I was into, but enough to be concerned. And I'm sure my complete disregard for life during this season had them worried.

When I lost the bar, I lost my identity. That's the danger in allowing what you do to become who you are. The truth is, no business, job, or life's work is as stable as we'd like it to be. Just because it's winning today doesn't guarantee it won't lose tomorrow. And when your identity is attached to highs and lows, your feelings, emotions, and family are affected by them. Real identity shouldn't be tied to things with no stability.

But mine was, and therefore, I had no idea who I was anymore. For months, I fell into a vicious cycle of depression. I had no job, which made me hate myself. And because I hated myself, I couldn't muster up the motivation to go and get a job. Finally, a friend tried to help me snap out of it. They put in a

Real identity shouldn't be tied to things with no stability.

good word for me at the restaurant they were employed at, and I got a job there as a server.

Going from hiring servers to being hired as one was a test that my pride wasn't ready to pass. I was good at the job, and I really needed it. But I also didn't care about it whatsoever.

In my depressed state, my drug usage had picked up drastically. I was still using Adderall, and a boatload of it. It was preventing me from sleeping and functioning as a healthy human. I also was using Xanax, an anti-anxiety drug, to try to bring me down enough to sleep. The two drugs were constantly combatting each other in my system. But I just continued to increase the dosage of both.

Just to be clear, by increase I mean I was taking 4x the amount prescribed to any human.

It's also important to note that my gambling addiction hadn't gone away. Addiction is super abusive like that. It doesn't leave you alone, even once it's beaten you up and taken everything of value from you. The job as a server provided the money I needed to go to the casino which kept the taste of gambling in my mouth. However, it wasn't nearly enough to satisfy my appetite.

I stole money from the restaurant so I could place larger bets. I got caught and was fired. Again. And I was so depressed that I didn't care. I went on to be fired from two more meaningless jobs for stealing. Since I wasn't intentional about my identity, I just accepted who I had become. I was a depressed addict and thief. Since stealing from jobs wasn't working out, I decided to try stealing from cars.

On the night I stole a vehicle, I was feeling exceptionally low and desperate. The Adderall in my system wouldn't let me fall asleep. It had me fully alert at 3 in the morning. In fact, I hadn't slept for days, and my brain was starting to betray me because of the lack of rest. Thoughts of anxiety, depression, and self-hate were running through my mind. I had to do something, anything, to get them to stop. I knew the only hope of relief, even if temporary, would be found at the casino. But to go to the casino, I needed some cash.

That's how I found myself roaming around my parents' apartment complex, checking to see if any cars were unlocked. I was hoping to find purses or wallets left inside. I'd even settle for valuable items that I could sell for gambling money. I struck out car after car until finally, I hit the jackpot—an unlocked 1999 Buick LeSabre (pretty lame, I know).

I opened up the door and looked around. There was no wallet, purse, or anything of significant value at first glance. But when I lifted up the console, I found something better than I ever could have dreamt. The owner left *the keys* inside the car.

There's nothing that excuses what I did next. But I'm telling the truth when I say I never set out to steal a car. I was comfortable stealing from registers, but grand theft auto was a different story. Only crazy people would do that, or so I thought.

My decision making was so messed up from the drugs and my downward spiral that I actually *thought* the keys were a gift. Maybe even from God himself. As I held them in my hand, a rush of adrenaline ran through my body. I felt the weight of the moment settle on my shoulders. Was I going to take advantage of this unexpected opportunity? With no consideration of any consequence, the answer to that question became a resounding yes.

I stuck the keys in the ignition and drove away. Although I had obviously driven many times before, this was a drive like I had never experienced before. It was nerve-racking but also exhilarating. I felt uneasy and hopeful at the same time. But the amazing thing was, I actually felt something. My depression had deprived me of feeling for so long that I decided this was a high worth riding.

I had a friend who promised me I could come to stay with him in Houston, and he would help me start over. I hid the stolen car and walked home to pack. I gathered my belongings, told my parents someone was picking me up to drive me across the country, and I set out hoping for a brighter future. They didn't know what was going on, and this was the first time they'd seen any sort of ambition out of me in months. I'm sure they were skeptical, but they also knew they didn't know how to help me. So they let me go without argument and hoped for the best.

I made it all the way to Cheatham County, Tennessee. Since I had now been up for three days straight, I knew I needed to sleep. I didn't want to show up at my friends looking like a zombie. He knew I had hit a rough patch but was unaware of the depths of my problems. So I pulled into the parking lot of a laundromat in the small town of Ashland City. I dozed off for a few hours and woke up to...

Well, you know the rest of the story. I was pulled out of the car, yelled at, handcuffed, and arrested.

My decisions led me to a place in life that I never anticipated being. In the back of a cop car. And not because I got pulled over for speeding and forgot my license. Or even for getting busted drinking and driving. Nope. Because I stole a car and drove it across the country.

The truth is, stealing the car wasn't the reason I ended up where I had. Sure, it was the decision that led me to get arrested. But there were all sorts of small decisions beforehand that led me to that place. The decisions to drink excessively, do drugs, gamble, steal from the bar, take from other restaurants, and not deal with any of my issues internally all led me to this point.

I didn't steal the car because I was a person who loved stealing cars. Instead, I stole it because I wanted to run away from my past. Speaking literally, I tried to drive away from it. Really, really far away. But that's the thing about problems that aren't dealt with. No matter how far you go or how fast you run, your problems will always catch up to you.

Starting Over vs. Running Away.

Looking back, I probably should have stolen something nicer than a 1999 Buick LeSabre. The moment I held the keys to that car in my hands. I recognized it as an opportunity, which, on one end, was actually true. However, I was incorrect about what type of opportunity it was. I thought it was an opportunity to start over when it was actually an opportunity to run away.

Many people don't realize this, but starting over and running away are two completely different things. They can easily seem identical at first, so let's dive into what makes them unique.

Starting over is beginning a new opportunity with new surroundings all while working through your issues. Sometimes new surroundings are beneficial and even necessary. New opportunities and friends can be helpful to help you heal and move forward toward healthy things. Starting over can be a good or even a great decision!

At first glance, running away seems like the same thing. It's also choosing to begin a new opportunity with new surroundings. However, you run away with the intention of not facing any problems. Running away happens when you're not looking to heal or become healthy, just escape.

Moving to Houston wasn't a bad thing. But stealing a car to get there was. Not getting help with my drug or gambling addiction was. Not talking to anybody about my depression was. Developing a habit of stealing from those around me was. If I was interested in starting over, I would have taken a step toward processing and healing from those things. But I wasn't interested in real change, I just wanted to escape.

Here's one of the biggest things I learned from stealing that car. And I think it's so crucial for those of you heading toward your comeback and real, sustainable change in your life.

Problems travel with you until you face them.

It doesn't matter how far you go. It doesn't matter how good the new situation seems to be. It doesn't matter if you don't know anybody in the new town you move to or the job you start. It doesn't even matter if you cut ties with the people who know your deepest, darkest secrets.

Your problems travel with you even when they're

Stop focusing so much on your surroundings and start focusing on yourself.

uninvited. They don't require you to pack them in a suitcase to still make the trip. Most issues are internal, which means wherever you go, you bring them with you.

My problems caught up to me in Tennessee, and I'm actually thankful they did sooner rather than later. Because the truth is, they would have found me in Houston, too. It wouldn't have been long before I started ruining job opportunities, stealing from my friend, and gambling away all of my money there. Internal problems aren't altered by external things.

Wherever you go, you take you with you. That's why I'd challenge you to stop focusing so much on the surroundings and start focusing on yourself.

You can become a better person, student, spouse, or parent. And when you change, a world of new possibilities become available to you.

Facing Fear.

The reason most of us never face our problems is that we're afraid of them. It's always easier to suppress a problem and ignore it. But every time you hide an issue, it pops back up with more complications, ready to ruin your life in new, creative ways.

Like a collections company that always finds a way to get ahold of you. (I've had to change my number so many times)

The longer we keep problems hidden, the longer they have power over us. Our minds trick us into believing that our issues are scarier than they actually are. It's when we finally expose our problems, that we can take back power over them. Power to actually deal with them. Only what we reveal, can be healed.

I'm not saying overcoming your problems will be easy or fast. In fact, I can almost guarantee you that it will be hard and take longer than you'd like. I know that because we'd all like our problems fixed instantly! I'm simply saying there's a shift that happens as soon as you start living in freedom. Working on you makes you feel better about you.

I was forced to stop using drugs cold turkey when I went to jail. I remember the nurse asking me how I was feeling. And even though my body was experiencing some withdrawals, I remember it felt so good to talk about my addiction problems with somebody openly. It was the first time I ever had.

As I expressed to her the freedom I experienced in that moment, she smiled and shared that many people before me had the same feeling. When you get used to suppressing, hiding, and running from problems your whole life, something special happens when you face them.

What problems do you currently have? Are you addicted, anxious, depressed, insecure, financially unstable, overweight, or unfaithful to a spouse? Here's what I know:

The freedom that comes from facing your problems is greater than the fear you currently feel.

The most significant progress in life always lies on the other side of fear. If you're going to change, fear is something you have to face. But together, we can look it in the face and let it know that we will overcome it. It's not bigger than you, you're bigger than it!

Comeback Challenge.

I want you to experience the same freedom I did in the nurse's room that day. Unfortunately for me, I didn't choose to face my problems; I was forced to. But you have the opportunity right now to decide to face your problems rather than being forced into it. And trust me, there are fewer repercussions that way. Here's your comeback challenge for this chapter: **Talk to somebody about your problems.**

I'm not saying pick a random stranger or someone who has the same issues as you. Instead, choose someone who you can trust and has your best interest in mind. And talk to them about what you're dealing with. It's the first step in facing your problems!

I'm not promising that confession will make all your problems go away, but I promise you'll feel freedom when it's out in the open. And once you can see your problems from a perspective of freedom, you can keep taking the necessary steps to defeat it.

Start small. Build up the muscle of getting things out there. But at least start somewhere. Your comeback depends on you dealing with your problems.

Bonus Challenge.

Similar to Chapter 4, I want to hear your story! Go to **youllneverchange.com/story** and share how you're starting to face your fears. It's a big deal and you deserve some recognition.

Seven.

GOD DOESN'T CARE

"I WANNA TALK TO GOD BUT I'M AFRAID 'CAUSE WE AIN'T SPOKE IN SO LONG"
[KANYE WEST]

It turns out when you break the law and get arrested, you actually go to jail. Growing up, I viewed jail as a place reserved for the scumbags of society. It not only punished those who deserved it but kept the rest of us "good people" protected. Even when I was stealing money and cars, I never considered I'd end up there. I was delusional and thought I was above repercussions.

As it turns out, I was wrong, no surprise. I spent six months of my life in Cheatham County Jail. Some of you reading this are no strangers to jail and are educated on how the process works. I know because I wrote this book with you in mind. But for those of you who are strangers to jail, I want to make sure you stay unfamiliar with it. Let me explain how it works, so you don't have to experience it to understand.

Jail is a holding place for those charged with a crime who haven't yet been sentenced. During your court case, a judge can assign you to prison. Jail and prison are two different places.

I spent six months in jail awaiting my day in court. After my court date the judge gave me two years probation, which I could serve in Ohio, with a charge of felony theft over $1,000. The time I spent in jail made me very thankful I did no additional time. Here's what an average day looked like…

I didn't have my own cell as you often see on TV. Instead, I shared what's called a pod with twenty other guys. Imagine living in a huge locker room that you'd find in an outdated middle school. There were no decorations, floor rugs, lava lamps, or anything to make the atmosphere feel even the slightest bit cozy. Day after day, you'd try to find solace staring at the bright white cinder block walls.

The pod was an open floor plan with ten bunk beds, three tables, a two toilets, and one TV. There was no "me time" or place where you could escape. You got used to using the bathroom in front of people real quick.

When you're in jail your life revolves around food. You don't get very much and can only eat at certain times. Even though the food is TERRIBLE, it was the only thing you had to look forward to. The guards woke you up at 6am for breakfast. The 5 star chefs that worked there didn't like variety very much, as it was always dry oatmeal, droopy eggs, and OJ out of a cardboard box. For lunch, two pieces of bread with a slice of bologna in the middle would be dropped off for you at your pod at 12pm. I would call it a sandwich, but that wouldn't do a real sandwich any sort of justice. The red drink they served did have some redeeming qualities. If you used your imagination it sorta tasted like kool-aid minus the sugar. I looked forward to the evenings, because dinner was the only food variety of the day. I'd always hope for beans and cornbread. It was the only thing that actually filled me up.

When you weren't eating, there were three things to do. You could play cards, watch TV, or tell stories. Every pod had unofficially appointed someone to be the pod-father (yes, like the God-father) who was in charge. He made the crucial decisions of what card games would be played and what channels would be watched. We were a sports and sitcom kind of group.

Storytelling was my personal favorite activity. The rest of my pod mates had lived in Tennessee their whole lives. (You could tell by country accents) Compared to everyone else there I didn't quite fit the typical jail stereotype, although I did get a tattoo while I was there. Bonus points because it says "mom". But since I was from Ohio and had different experiences, I gained popularity by telling my stories. And being respected is a good thing in jail.

The reason I'm telling you all of this is so you can get a picture of how unglamorous jail really is. If the most exciting parts of your day are telling stories and eating beans, then your day isn't all that exciting. And all I had was time on my hands to reflect.

As I reflected, I realized I had done things I never thought I would do. I never expected to be an addict who tried to steal my way out of every bad situation I created. I had aspirations and even success at some of the things I pursued! I never expected to be in jail and had no idea how I became a person awaiting a trial.

There was one thought that kept playing in my head. That said, *how did I get here*? And even though it was important to answer, it felt impossible. Because to answer it, I had to face myself. And truthfully, I hated myself. I made selfish decisions that hurt and disappointed those closest to me.

As you continue to read my story, you'll discover that jail became a major turning point in my life. It wasn't until I faced the person I became that I could change. There were a few things that happened in jail that empowered me to confront myself.

The first was a letter I received from my mom during my first month in jail.

All life transitions are challenging, whether it be a new school, job, or place of residence. Trying to adjust to something new can feel uncomfortable and difficult. Trying to process jail as your new reality is especially problematic because it was a transition you didn't choose or expect. Sure, you made the decisions to get there. But you usually don't weigh the consequences of your choices until you have to face them. For me, going to sleep behind bars in a jail jumpsuit brought overwhelming feelings of shame and guilt that first month. (I still refuse to wear the color orange to this day, ask my wife)

I assumed my friends and family hated me and were done with me. I figured that my family had probably disowned me. I hadn't become the son they had raised me to be. That's why getting a letter from my mom was such a big deal. And I'll be honest, it wasn't a "feel good" letter. While she mentioned that she loved me, she also talked a lot about how disappointed she was. But the fact that she cared enough to write a letter at all did wonders for my self-esteem. She wouldn't have told me to "get my crap together" if she didn't believe I actually could.

The second significant moment in jail was a "church service". Now when I say church service, you might think of a room fully set up with a stage, audio equipment, and plenty of seats to host a large crowd. Your perception of the space is dependent on if you've been to a church that's more modern or traditional. Either way, this service looked nothing like the picture you probably have in your head.

Service was held in a tiny, claustrophobic room with fourteen chairs set up in a circle. There was no stage, no audio equipment, and barely enough room. There were way too many of us circled around an old man with an old, out-of-tune guitar.

As we got started, I remember he strummed the guitar a few times and tuned it up. He then said, "Well, fellas, this is an oldie but a goodie." And he proceeded to play the song Amazing Grace.

I was familiar with the old hymn from church. But for those of you who are unfamiliar, here's the chorus of the song written in 1772 by John Collins:

Amazing grace! How sweet the sound
That saved a wretch like me.
I once was lost, but now am found,
Was blind but now I see.[1]

There was something special about hearing a roomful of men who had ended up in jail sing about being saved, found, and seeing clearly again. And what led them to that place? God's amazing grace.

I didn't fully understand what was happening at that moment, but I felt a weight lift off of me for the first time in years. I shed a few tears, even though you weren't supposed to cry in jail. And I cannot fully explain it, but I had an overwhelming sense that everything would be okay. I didn't even have the understanding to equate that feeling to God showing up, but He did.

The truth was, nothing about my situation had changed. I had become an addict, thief, was in jail and awaiting a court date. I had screwed over some of the most important people to me. My life was a mess. But God was pursuing me in the middle of that mess. And whenever God shows up, he always brings his grace

What mess are you in right now? Maybe your situation isn't as bad as mine, or perhaps it's even worse. I don't know what you've done or who you've become. But I do know this…

There's no mess that grace won't get in the middle of. Your comeback requires grace for yourself, and lots of it.

Amazing Grace.

My definition of grace is favor that is unexpected or undeserved. Grace isn't something that can be "earned," but only ever given. It can come in the form of a spouse, child, friendship, house, opportunity, or fresh start.

My jail mates singing about "being saved" while simultaneously locked behind bars every night was a product of grace. Their external circumstances kept them imprisoned. But internally, they found freedom through God.

Me feeling a weight lifted off my shoulders during that church service was a product of grace. I wasn't looking, asking, or expecting for that to happen. The truth is, I only went to the service so that I could escape my pod for a few hours. It was unexpected and undeserved, but it still happened.

I know we haven't talked a lot about faith in this book. And I know that all of you reading this might have different thoughts or experiences with God. I'm not here to tell you what to believe but in full transparency, even when I didn't believe in God, grace still showed up in my life.

A lot of times, grace looks like forgiveness. Forgiveness happens when someone chooses to not hold an offense against the offender. It doesn't erase what happened, but it allows the offender to move forward.

God made it apparent to me in that tiny, white-walled cinder block room that he forgave me for my offenses. I still had to face the repercussions of them, but I also had the freedom to move past them. But even when God forgives you, the bigger challenge is forgiving yourself.

His forgiveness eventually led me to a place where I could forgive myself. And whether you believe in God or not, the principle of grace still holds true for you. You can't change until you give yourself grace.

I know what you're thinking. *But Nate, I don't deserve it.* Honestly, you're right. You don't. But that's what grace is— unexpected and undeserved favor. People who won't forgive themselves have low self-esteem. They think they aren't worth anything, including change. Change requires that you value yourself enough to give grace to yourself.

The most valuable thing I learned while in jail. And whether you're in actual jail, or simply imprisoned by your past, you need this to move forward: If you never forgive the old you, the new you doesn't stand a chance to exist.

Let me speak directly to you for a second. You've done some bad things. You've made some serious mistakes. Maybe you've stolen, cheated, lied, and worried your way into becoming someone you never thought you'd be. Regardless, here's what I believe. What you did is not who you are. Accept grace, and it's amazing gift to move forward.

If you never forgive the old you, the new you doesn't stand a chance to exist.

Talking to Yourself.

Even though grace is unearned, and therefore always available, we must be careful to not take advantage of it. It doesn't lend itself to us to make the same mistakes without having to change. Grace should serve as the foundation of your fresh start. It's the place you can start to build the new you from.

When I experienced grace in a real way that day, I realized I didn't want to be the old Nate anymore. I developed an understanding that I was more valuable than the life I had created. I had optimism that I could stop tearing down the people around me and start building them up. I actually began to look at jail as an opportunity to finish writing my story the right way, so someday I could share it with someone who needed it.

As I thought about my life, I could almost visualize three versions of myself. There was the present me, who had to decide who he wanted to be going forward. There was the past me, who made some serious mistakes. And there was also the future me, who was excited about who he could become. It was as if the past and future me were playing tug-of-war with the present me, trying to win me over to their side.

It helped me to categorize and visualize these three parts of myself. We all have a past and future us fighting for our surrender in the here and now. And the side we choose to give in to every day determines whether we will move forward or backward.

I decided to have conversations with those three parts of me. I'd encourage you to do the same. By the way, if talking to yourself out loud makes you feel crazy, feel free to keep those conversations in your head. As you can probably already tell from this book, I'm not afraid to get a little crazy.

But let's go through the three conversations we need to be having with ourselves as we're undergoing the process of change. Hope you have that highlighter.

First, there's the conversation with the past you. The most important thing you can say to the past you is, "I forgive you and I love you." You can't excuse all the mistakes you've made, but you also can't hate yourself because of them. Forgiveness and acceptance release the past you from self-hatred and since self-hatred always leads to self-sabotage, only self-love can destroy the lie that says you're too far gone. Love makes you better. So you only get better by learning to love yourself.

Second, there's the conversation with the present you. The most important thing you can say to the present you is, "I believe in you." If you're having a conversation with the present you, it's confirmation that you're making progress. The desire for change is proof you're heading in the right direction. You have to coach yourself, because there may be nobody else there to coach you. People won't believe you can change because they won't yet see you changing. Why? Because change is always internal before it's external. That's why it's crucial to encourage the present you for trying.

Lastly, there's the conversation with future you. The most important thing you can say to the future you is, "I promise I'll do whatever it takes." The healthy vision you have of your future you is the version of you that you deserve. It's also the version of you those around you need. It's a person that will contribute to the world in significant ways. Promising the future you that you're fighting for them to eventually become the present you is so powerful!

Do you want to change? Then forgive the past you, believe in the present you, and make promises to the future you.

Comeback Challenge.

I'm going to end this chapter by challenging you to have the conversations you need with the past you. I say conversations because it's not going to be one and done. You will have to have these conversations consistently in order to begin believing it. Here's the challenge: **Look yourself in the mirror, think of everything you've done wrong, and start forgiving yourself.**

What would your life look like if you could forgive yourself? You don't have to live bound up by shame and guilt. You don't have to accept the things you've done as who you are. You don't have to allow self-hatred to define the quality of your life and prevent you from moving forward.

And once you forgive the past you, believe in the present you as you start to transform into your vision of the future you. You can change! But your comeback requires you to go back and forgive the past you.

Bonus Challenge.

Do you want to know more about Faith and what I believe about God? Go to **youllneverchange.com/faith**. I'd love to share my heart with you.

Eight.

THEY'LL NEVER TRUST ME AGAIN

"THEY SAID I WOULDN'T BE NOTHING, NOW THEY ALWAYS SAY CONGRATULATIONS"
[POST MALONE]

For the first seven chapters of this book, we've done an in-depth dive into the biggest mistakes I made in my life. In reality it probably could have been 15 chapters. The lessons I shared with you so far didn't hit me when they happened because I wasn't actively pursuing change. I apply those principles now, but it might have saved me a lot of pain if I was aware enough to recognize them back then. I hope you can see where my mistakes led me, so yours don't have to lead you to a similar place.

Jail was the turning point for me. That's where I decided that I needed to change, wanted to change, and became determined to change. It was the starting place of my comeback. I share this because I think it's important that we're on the same page regarding how my comeback worked. Once I decided that I wanted to change, I started applying wise principles to my life proactively instead of simply learning them reactively. (wax on wax off)

Life is the best teacher out there. Through our experiences, victories, defeats, pursuits, and pain, there's so much we can learn every single day. And while the lessons life has to offer us are significant, we only change if we take them and start proactively applying them to our futures.

Let's turn the corner and start the journey through my comeback…

I got out of jail with two years of felony probation that

was to be served in Ohio. So, upon my release, I had to figure out how to make my way back home. Can you guess where I was going to live? Yup. Back in with mom and dad again! If you're counting, this is the third time.

I seriously am forever grateful to my parents for not giving up on me. They never stopped loving me as their son regardless of how many times I got it wrong. And because they loved me, they continued to open their doors to me again and again. They even sent me some money to afford a bus ticket for the long ride back home to Ohio.

The first night out of jail felt terrific. Directly after my release, I stopped at a Walgreens to use the restroom. When I walked through the door, the lady working at the counter asked me if she could help me find anything. She also called me honey, as you'd expect from a middle-aged southern woman. I know she was simply doing her job by asking me if I needed help, but I could feel a few tears roll down my cheek. It had been so long since somebody had actually cared about me. I forgot what being treated as a valuable human being felt like.

When I finally got back home, my mom made the whole family a celebratory meal. It wasn't anything fancy, just some good old-fashioned grilled chicken. The amount of flavor that my taste buds picked up was unreal! I remember thinking my mom was a gourmet chef. I repeatedly told her she didn't have to spoil me like that! It was a big step up from bologna bread and watered down red drink.

As the honeymoon of freedom started to wear off, there were some real-life things I had to face. But the good thing about hitting rock bottom is you've already experienced the worst. Fear doesn't grip you in the same way when you know the only direction you can travel is up.

I needed to start with finding a job. It's no surprise that wasn't a super easy thing to do with my work history of stealing from employers and recent jail time. I had a pretty realistic understanding that I wasn't going to step right back into helping somebody run their business or manage people.

During college, I spent my summers landscaping for a local company. I decided to reach out to my old boss, even though I was surprisingly afraid to do so. I guess deep down, I really cared what people thought about me. Confessing about my time in jail was humiliating and required uncomfortable honesty, but it was also healthy. You can never move forward into your future without owning your past.

You can never move forward into your future without owning your past.

My boss was gracious enough to give me a chance, which is important to take note of. Most of the time, we build a narrative in our heads about how people will respond to our past, which keeps us from living openly. But the truth is, the worst-case scenario rarely comes true. And even when it does, it doesn't hurt you to the level you thought it would. There's a support system out there that believes in your comeback and is willing to help!

I worked for the landscaping company that whole summer. Since I was the newest employee, I was the low man on the totem pole. I became the grunt laborer that every landscaping crew needs. I spent every hour of every day weed whacking. That way, the top dogs could breeze through on their fancy mowers without having to worry about the tight spaces. But weed whacking wasn't even the most embarrassing part of the whole setup.

My parents had moved out of the apartment complex I stole the car from. So up until this point, I had been avoiding going out that way. But surprisingly enough, that complex was on the list of properties that our landscaping company serviced regularly. I spent an entire day there every single week. It was embarrassing, and I always was overly alert of people noticing me, even though nobody probably did. But it ended up being an uncomfortable, good thing. It forced me to face my past as a new man—one who wasn't stealing to support his addiction but working to support his new life.

The landscaping job wasn't just awkward; it was hard work. And for very little pay! But at this point in my life, it was the second-best thing that ever happened to me, right after going to jail.

The benefits of it seem simple and maybe even insignificant. Most of the time, the things that create real, sustainable change in our lives do.

That job forced me to wake up early every single morning and go to work. I laid out my clothes every night and made sure my laundry got done. I planned my meals and packed my lunch. People counted on me, even though it was for something simple.

Landscaping provided consistency for me. It was huge because my life had been inconsistent for so long. I was so used to harmful escapes, like getting high. Structuring my life around work proved I could intentionally direct my efforts toward something positive. I had become accustomed to screwing people over and letting them down. But coming through day after day for those who were counting on me felt good.

On the journey to my comeback, I just decided I was willing to start at the bottom. Even further, I committed to giving the bottom everything I had. And the consistency I developed in that season is the consistency that still carries me through every day.

Consistency isn't flashy. It doesn't look sexy to the people around you. It doesn't even always feel good in the moment. But it works. And when you become a consistent person, your life will inevitably change.

Day After Day.

My definition of consistency is what you repeatedly do. By repeatedly, I mean day after day after day after day. The biggest test of consistency is our feelings. When you choose to do the same thing repeatedly, even when you don't feel like it, you prove that you're a consistent person.

Truthfully, I didn't feel like waking up and weed whacking every morning that summer. Most days, my feelings screamed not to. Maybe you know what it's like to have your feelings grab your attention with temptations that are counter-productive to the consistency you're developing.

Sleep past your alarm.
You're too tired for work.
This job isn't leading you anywhere, anyways.
That person is annoying, cancel your meeting with them.
A couple of cookies won't hurt.
Just one hit, you'll feel better.

We choose to stay rooted in consistency when where we want to go becomes more important than how difficult it may be to get there. If landscaping taught me one thing, it's this: Consistency creates credibility.

Credibility happens when you become a person who does what you say you're going to do. It's the trust that's formed, shaped, and molded by your consistent actions. Credibility is a non-negotiable if you're going to go anywhere in life.

I know you might push back and wonder why it was important for me to become a credible person in the landscaping company's eyes. I get it. Landscaping wasn't the direction my life was heading. The place I work at now, never called my landscaping boss as a reference.

Consistency creates credibility.

It wasn't about proving my credibility to the landscaping company as much as it was about proving credibility to myself. Accepting a new identity as a credible person was a huge deal for me. Now, I have the credibility to influence hundreds of people every week. But it started by the consistency of picking up a weed whacker every day, even when it was the last thing I felt like doing.

When I look in the mirror now, I'm still far from perfect. But I do know I'm credible. I do what I say, I show up on time, and I don't lie about what I'm doing.

We must become a credible person before we can build the life we want. It's the foundation that stabilizes everything. And that foundation is created through the process of consistency.

The Hardest 4 Letter Word.

One of the biggest enemies to consistency is the myth of instant gratification. We all have dreams, goals, and vision of what we'd like our lives to look like. (Here's your reminder to finish chapter 2's challenge) You could probably paint a picture of the impact you want to make on the world and the lifestyle it would produce. And it seems so appealing that you probably want it now.

Have you ever looked at somebody else's success before? It always seems like it happened overnight. We think that people's charisma somehow magically elevated them to the top and it seems unfair. Why is that?

When we look at success, we don't consider the process. We weren't apart of it. So we see the finished product but never feel the pain they went through to get there. We don't consider that they did the right things repeatedly to get to that point.

While it's true that some get where they're headed faster than others, I don't know of anyone who reached their goals in the absence of process. The truth is, most success stories took years to write. And that leads us to the hardest four-letter word to digest on the planet. It's spelled w-a-i-t.

Nobody wants to wait. But if you can't wait, and be consistent while you are, you'll never create your comeback. It's easy to be consistent at anything for a few days, but days don't change you. Months and years do.

Anyone can diet for a few days, but you'll shed some serious pounds if you stick to your diet for a year.

Your spouse will be thankful if you take them on one date, but your marriage will change if you take them on one every other week.

You can guilt yourself to stay sober for 30 days, but your life will change forever if you stay sober for 30 years.

Everybody has a business idea, but few are willing to continue working on it when it's not working yet.

We tend to change the method but rarely is it the actual problem. What do I mean? We trade one diet for another, one rehab center for another, one romance for another, or one career for another. Changing the method will only lead us to the same problem in a different context. Long term consistency, in the same direction, is what produces real change.

Our goals require waiting. Furthermore, they require that we be consistent in the waiting. Where you are today isn't where you'll be forever if you stay consistent. Who I was, is not who I am today.

Comeback Challenge.

What's something that's right in front of you that you can do an excellent job at? It may not feel like much. But regardless of how small it seems, there's nothing to be embarrassed about. It might be a part-time job, recovery meetings, your business that isn't off the ground yet, a spouse to take care of, or children to love. Regardless of what it is, here's your comeback challenge: **Write down what you can be consistent with right now.**

What does that look like for your life? If you work at McDonald's, show up to work five minutes early and treat every customer with excellent customer service, even if they're not nice themselves. If you're a husband, plan a date for your wife every other week, even if it's as simple as bringing home a movie. If you're a business owner, hop on a coaching call every single month. It's not as much about what you do, but that you do it consistently. You'll figure out the right things to do along the way.

Bonus Challenge.

Everyone deserves another chance. If you haven't checked out the 30 day challenge yet, here's another opportunity.

The 30 day challenge is focused on helping you make new decisions and staying consistent. I want you to be apart of this challenge and hear from those who've already done it, go to **youllneverchange.com/challenge**.

Nine.

I CAN'T DO THIS

"I'M STANDING UP, I'MMA FACE MY DEMONS, I'M MANNING UP, I'MMA HOLD MY GROUND"
[EMINEM]

A few months into landscaping, I felt myself growing stagnant. Staying out of trouble was a big win for me. Obviously, I was coming out of a season defined by the chaos I stirred up. But on the other hand, I didn't really know what I was moving toward. The landscaping job was developing some positive things internally, but I didn't want to be there forever.

The physical labor aspect of the job beat me up pretty good, leaving me exhausted every day. It's amazing how heavy a weed whacker gets after a few hours. So every night I came home, I'd go straight to the spare bedroom I was sleeping in at my parents' house. It was an old laundry room converted into a bedroom. There was only enough space for my bed and a dresser. If you've ever watched Harry Potter, it was very much like him sleeping underneath the staircase.

In my experience landscaping and smoking weed go hand in hand. This isn't the case for all landscapers but it was for me. I got big into smoking weed in that season, which was risky given my history of addiction. And oh yeah, I also was on probation. But I figured since I wasn't doing hard drugs, I was making progress. Nobody changes entirely overnight, even when they're taking steps in the right direction.

The combination of being exhausted from my job and smoking weed every day put me in a very mellowed-out state. I laid in my bed like a zombie for hours on end, watching YouTube.

While it wasn't very productive, it did keep me from gambling, stealing, or any other stupid thing I could have been doing.

I remember coming across a promo video for the huge Floyd Mayweather versus Conor McGregor fight that was about to go down in a few months. I wasn't much of a boxing fan, but the way they put this promo together could have drawn anybody in. Motivational music, clips of them punching the bag, and some fire one liners will get anybody's adrenaline pumping.

For those of you who don't know much about the fight, let me catch you up to speed.

The year was 2017. Floyd Mayweather was, and still is, arguably the best boxer of all time. (Don't @ me) He retired with a record of 49-0 two years earlier. But he agreed to put his undefeated record on the line and come back to box against Conor McGregor.

Conor McGregor wasn't a professional boxer, but a UFC fighter. UFC is full-body fighting, with punches, kicks, and chokeholds. It's a match made in heaven for the men out there born with too much testosterone. Conor was the best in the sport at that time, with a record of 21-3 headed into the fight. Even though he wasn't a boxer, he had unmatched confidence and deep-down aggression never before seen.

The fight was historically hyped up because of the storylines. It was the first time ever a UFC fighter and boxer were going head to head. Floyd's 49-0 record was on the line. Conor was talking smack like nobody's business. The two seemed to hate each other. Oh yeah, they both walked away with their share of $410 Million. Not a bad payday![1]

This fight started to draw me in hardcore. I watched every video I could find. My favorite became one about Conor's backstory, mostly because I related to him. He wasn't a prodigy growing up and didn't come from much. But he prided himself on believing in his ability when nobody else did. He committed to continuing to learn, give it everything he had, and move forward.

He started from nothing and became the most successful fighter in his sport. He was even confident enough to switch sports and go punch for punch with the greatest boxer in history. I felt like my life was starting at nothing, as well. And even though I hadn't made anything of myself yet, his confidence started to become contagious. I wanted what he had.

That video really started my personal development journey. There was a correlation between the content I consumed and the motivation I began to feel. Positive content produced positive thoughts. And positive thoughts led to positive actions.

I started consuming as much personal developmental content as I could. I took advantage of the hours I spent landscaping by listening to audiobooks and podcasts. I learned from the comeback stories of others. I started to become educated on how to become spiritually, financially, and physically healthy. I'd listen to an entire book in a single day about how to become successful in fields that lined up with my dreams and skills.

It was in that season that I started to become ambitious. And when ambition is supported by empowerment, your actions begin to change. I decided I would take one year and become the best I could be at every area in my life. I worked hard at becoming a better son by investing in my relationship with my parents. I made a lot of progress in my health by going to the gym and cleaning up my diet consistently. I grew spiritually by going to church every Sunday and reading the Bible on my own.

I set the crazy goal of making $100,000 by the end of that year. I wanted to use it to pay back everyone I had stolen from. Let me be very clear. That never came close to happening. My online drop shipping business didn't take off the way I had hoped, as they inevitably never do. But the point is, my apathy turned into ambition. And for the first time in my life, I was ambitious for the right things.

I credit a lot of that to the content I was consuming. The truth is, what you put in matters. Positive voices get you thinking in a positive direction. But the opposite is also true. Negative voices make you think in a negative direction, even if you don't realize it.

Everything we consume develops us. And what we consume determines which direction we develop in.

Wisdom In, Wisdom Out.

Generally speaking, we know that whatever goes in usually comes out. For example, whenever you put gas in your car, it comes out as energy that powers your vehicle.

It works the same way with wisdom, which leads us to the biggest thing I learned during the personal development season of my life:

When wisdom goes in, wisdom comes out.

To truly understand this concept, we must develop an understanding of what wisdom is. Here's how Google defines it: "The soundness of an action or decision with regard to the application of experience, knowledge, and good judgment."[2]

Wisdom helps us to order our lives in a way that's sound. If you've ever been around a wise person, it seems as if they always know the right things to do at the right moments. It stems from them applying lessons from their past experiences,

Everything we consume develops us. And what we consume determines which direction we develop in.

the knowledge they've accumulated, and good judgment to their lives. Don't you hate those people!

I like to look at wisdom as "hidden knowledge." What do I mean by that? It's things we learn that aren't always natural to our humanity or evident to our minds. If you can dig out nuggets of wisdom and apply them to your life, you will live differently than the average human being. You'll also win at the things that really matter.

One of the most encouraging things about wisdom is that it's available to anyone. You just have to be willing to pursue it. Through people in your life, books, podcasts, YouTube, and various other sources in the modern-day world, it's out there! So why do such few people ever pursue it?

The starting place of wisdom is humility. To become wise, it begins with you admitting that you don't know everything. Because of my pride, that was actually a hard pill for me to swallow. You must have a willingness to challenge the mindsets that have gotten you to where you are. Getting unstuck only happens by doing things differently. And it's essential to learn the right things to do.

When you commit to becoming a lifetime learner, you position yourself well for wisdom. My guess is you'll eventually find it. However, the source you go to for the wisdom you need is important. Let me give you my "wisdom warning," which I suppose is actually wisdom in and of itself.

Only take advice from people you want to be like. The source is important whenever deciding what content will shape you. If it's someone you want to be like, at least in their area of expertise, then listen to what they have to say and shape your actions around their words. But if someone who doesn't have the type of life you desire tells you what to do, the best thing you can do is say "thank you" and move on.

Here are a few examples:

- You probably don't want relationship advice from your dad, who's been divorced three times.
- Your broke uncle shouldn't be the one telling you how to spend your money.
- Don't allow someone who doesn't have a business to shape your business plan.
- There are probably more credible podcasts on spirituality than those produced by the group of friends who have no pastoral experience.
- The personal trainer who has no muscle probably isn't the one you should work with if you're trying to get ripped.

The wisdom we apply guides the direction of our lives. So we must be critical about who we take it from. Don't hear me wrong, I believe that there's something we can learn from everybody. That's humility. But it's important to not allow humility to lead you into stupidity. Look at the contents of someone's life and ask yourself if you'd trade places with them. Listening to them will ensure you become like that. And who you become is an even more crucial part of your comeback than what you do.

John Maxwell says it best "Success has less to do with what you achieve and more to do with the person you become".

Comeback Challenge.

We've mentioned these sporadically throughout this chapter, but there are several places you can find wisdom. Here are the top ones, in my opinion.

A mentor. I guarantee they will change everything for you. We will talk about this more in the next chapter, but mentorship fast-tracked my comeback more than anything else. Mentors allow you to learn from their experiences rather than just yours. How great would it be to learn from someone else's mistakes instead of having to make them? This is the opportunity mentorship provides. We live in a society that has no shortage of content. But something special happens when you get face-to-face with somebody. You're not only learning from their words, but they provide crucial accountability and feedback, as well.

Books and Podcasts. I'll be honest, I'm not much of a reader. That's why this book is available in an audio version as well. But regardless of whether you learn by reading or listening, books are what people have learned over their entire lifetime condensed into a couple of hours. People share hours of their expertise on podcasts for no charge to you! If you want to learn, it's available. And for minimal cost.

YouTube. While school might be the primary education system in our world, I'm convinced that YouTube comes in a strong second. You can learn anything on there right now. I had a lawnmower that I didn't know how to start. I searched the model number on YouTube and ended up mowing the yard within a few minutes. When my wife found this out I lost the excuse of "I don't know how to do that". My point is, YouTube can be an incredible teacher in whichever subject you need to learn more about.

Now that you know where you can go to become wise, here's your comeback challenge: **What's your next book, podcast, or YouTube video you're watching?**

I'm thrilled you're reading this book. But if this is the last thing you do for your personal development, you're not going to go as far as you deserve in life. Choose an area you need to grow in, and pick out some content that can help. If you have people in your life that are continually growing, ask them what they recommend.

It might change your whole life, or it might not. But I bet it'll give you at least one tool that helps you along on your comeback journey.

Bonus Challenge.

The internet is a crazy place. Have you ever fallen into a YouTube black hole before? Where it's 3am and what you're bouncing between fail videos, cute cats, and flat earth?

I know how overwhelming it can be to figure out where to start, so I wanted to help. I consume a lot of content and I've gotten good at curating what's worth your attention. Every Monday I send out an email called "Wisdom" where I share the current book I'm reading, podcast I'm listening to, and YouTube video I'm watching. t it's important to not allow humility to lead you into stupidity. Look at the contents of someone's life and ask yourself if you'd trade places with them. Listening to them will ensure you become like that. And who you become is an even more crucial part of your comeback than what you do.

Go to **youllneverchange.com/wisdom** and let me help.

Ten.

I'M SICK OF FAKE FRIENDS

"BACK THEN THEY DIDN'T WANT ME, NOW I'M HOT THEY ALL UP ON ME"
[MIKE JONES]

After being inspired by Conor McGregor's comeback story, I started to take mine more seriously. I stopped living to simply "stay out of trouble" and started really thinking about who I wanted to become. Surviving was no longer enough. I had a deep desire to thrive.

If somebody with worse cards found a way to win, why couldn't I?

I noticed a common concept in other people's comeback stories. They each seemed to start with one crucial step. Surrounding themselves with the right people, so that's where I decided to start. I needed friends who had been to the next level and could help me get there, as well.

In the last chapter, we talked about the importance of wisdom. And while it was great to receive some inspiration from Conor McGregor's YouTube interviews, nothing replaces real relationships. So I started building relationships with people who were wise in the areas I wasn't. I had people who encouraged me in my health and others who held me accountable to my recovery. But I had one person in particular who I considered a mentor and accountability partner. He helped me grow spiritually, emotionally, and mentally. Overall, he led me down the challenging path of becoming a healthy and whole person. His name was Brad.

Brad and I went to church together as kids. I never would have thought I'd see him at the church I was checking out almost 10 years later. I did everything I could to avoid making eye contact or him recognizing me. Brad didn't know my story or what I had been through since the last time we hung out years ago. He was completely unaware of my bad choices, and probably even thought me incapable of making those kinds of mistakes.

You know that awkward moment when you see someone from your past and you don't know if they even remember you or if you should say anything so you just walk away? That was me. Let me give you some bonus advice… just go say hi, you'll feel better.

I'm thankful Brad didn't let that awkward moment pass. He stopped me, shook my hand, and expressed wanting to get coffee to catch up so we swapped numbers. I figured that a free cup of coffee was going to cost the pain of honesty, vulnerability, and quite possibly another ruined perception of me. But I needed a positive influence in my life.

I spilled my guts over that cup of coffee. It was the most real I had been with anyone in a long time. He listened patiently and calmly absorbed the shock of hearing about my addiction, car theft, and time in jail. At the end of my hour-long Starbucks rambling session, I asked him for help.

I didn't persuade him with a well-thought-out speech, and there was definitely nothing in it for him. But I learned a valuable lesson that day. There's power in asking someone for help. The truth is, everyone wants to feel valued. When you ask someone to help you, you're communicating that you respect and honor their character and accomplishment. Most of the time, if people can help, they want to. But unless you ask, you'll never know.

We scheduled a time to meet every week. In fact, we still do. That's the thing about mentorship. You never outgrow it or come to a place in life where it isn't needed. As soon as you do, you become stagnant. When you decide you don't want to learn anymore, you also indirectly decide to stop leveling up. Don't believe the lie, you can teach an old dog new tricks. How old are you? You can still learn.

Brad had a genuine care for me and where I was headed in life. Good mentors give advice from that place. And that sounds really nice, but honestly, it didn't always feel really nice. Why? Because love doesn't always feel good. Mentors speak to who you could become, not who you currently are. To reach potential, the present you must be pushed.

To reach potential, the present you must be pushed.

He challenged me week after week. It was never in a condemning way, but always gracious. I'm a firm believer you should only get a mentor if you're ready to be challenged. One of the biggest mistakes we can make is interpreting a challenge as condemnation. Even though they can be uncomfortable, challenges serve the purpose of building you up. Condemnation carries the intention of tearing you down.

I was always honest about where I was at. That included sharing my secret unhealthy thoughts I didn't want anybody to know about. It looked like being transparent when I slipped up and didn't get things right the previous week. Until you're ready to be honest about everything, a mentor won't do you much good. They can't help you fully unless they understand your situation completely.

The areas of my life that Brad and I worked on felt like a challenge to my manhood. I shared my feelings of self-hatred. This. Was. Not. Easy.

I shared some of my dreams with him that sounded stupid at the time. It's hard to open up about what you want to see out of your life before there's any progress in that direction. Insecurity will magnify the fear of someone else tearing your dream apart. And honestly, sometimes it felt like he was! But since he had experienced a level of success, he knew some of the right and wrong ways of approaching dreams. He helped me look past what I wanted to do and plan out how I would do it. He loved me enough to bring me back to reality so that I actually stood a chance of getting to where I wanted to go.

Maybe the most challenging advice to swallow was about one of my relationships. I remember I had told him about a girl I recently started dating, not really looking for advice, but just wanting to bring him in the loop. The truth was, we didn't start dating for the right reasons. I didn't see a future with this girl; I just wanted her to fill a void in my life and make myself feel better. Since Brad had a healthy marriage, he could see right through me. He responded by asking some tough questions. And I, of course, had no right answers.

"Are you going to marry this girl?" He asked, very directly.

"Uhhhhh…." I nervously tried to stall, knowing the answer but not wanting to admit it.

"Why are you wasting your time then?" He continued, "Do you think you're ready to date? You can't take care of somebody else until you're healthy, yourself. I promise you will be one day. But today is not that day."

In that same conversation, he told me to break up with her. I'd never had someone talk so much craziness and make so much sense at the same time. I was used to being in charge of my own love life. After all, it was my girlfriend. But do you know what I did? I broke up with her. I knew that my decisions had taken me to places I didn't want to go to. But Brad's decisions had taken him to where I eventually wanted to be. At the end of the day, it's pretty simple. If you want to walk in the direction of somebody else, make the similar decisions they did.

If you aren't going to take, internalize, and act on your mentor's advice, you're wasting time. Not just their time, but yours as well. They can give you the best advice in the world, but it won't work unless you grab ahold of it even when it doesn't make sense to you. It's often said that the most important thing you can have in any relationship is trust. Mentorship is no different. Results in your life are a product of you being willing to trust the wisdom of their life.

I'm so glad that I trusted my mentor enough to listen to his voice. The right voices in your life equal you making the right choices. But the opposite is also true. The wrong voices lead to the wrong choices.

I evaluated the contents of Brad's life and decided I wanted something similar. And I held onto that. His voice didn't always make sense to me. And it very rarely ever made me comfortable! But it did lead to the right choices. And when we make the right choices for a consistent period of time, we really do change.

The right voices in your life equal you making the right choices.

Friends = Future.

Do you remember elementary school? Our teachers taught us some valuable principles for life in that place when we were just kids. Honestly, if we would have absorbed them a little quicker, our lives would probably look slightly different. But better late than never!

The biggest lesson I learned in this season of mentorship was one that I failed to learn when it was taught in elementary school. I know it sounds basic, but life change isn't always complicated. It's about doing the right things, regardless of how basic they appear, over and over again. Here's the truth:

Your friends determine your future.

Sometimes as we get more driven and goal-oriented, it's easy to look past a "trivial" concept like friends. But our relationships matter, maybe more than anything else. Why? Because they determine the direction of our lives. Who we spend the most time with is who we inevitably become like.

My pride used to tell me that my friendships didn't matter. I thought I could hang out with whoever I wanted, whether it be party animals, drug addicts, or those with no ambition. As long as we got along, it was all good. I actually believed that I wasn't easily influenced. After all, I was a successful man. Therefore, I was strong enough to carve out my own path, I thought.

I sometimes look back on the course of my life and examine it. Every time I look at who I was during different seasons, I looked a lot like the people I was spending the most time with. Today, the same thing holds true. Jim Rohn says "You're the average of the five people you spend the most time with".

I got the chance to speak on this topic at a local recovery center. One of the guys attending the meeting raised his hand and shared some great perspective.

He talked about his experience being a contractor. A few years ago, he ran his own successful business, making more money than he had at any other point in his life. In that season, his community was primarily other contractors. They were people who were educated, successful, and driven. But then his life took a huge turn, he started smoking crack, and his entire community changed. He stopped hanging out with contractors and started spending time with addicts, drug dealers, and prostitutes.

He had a light bulb moment in the middle of my talk. He realized that his friends truly did determine his future.

When he stopped hanging out with contractors, he stopped making progress in contracting. When he started hanging out with drug dealers, he became a drug addict. He talked about the sad reality of losing his business, all of his money, and family. How could he have preserved his future? Choosing to do life with the right people. I hope you just had your own light bulb moment.

Can I encourage you for a second? Choose your friends wisely. I know it might take some patience for the right people to come into your life. It also might take you putting yourself out there and developing new relationships.

But here's the truth. The character of the five people you spend the most time with will shape you into what type of person you become. The positivity or negativity of your group will shape your life's outlook. You'll most likely make the average income of those who you're the closest. The health of your marriage will be determined by the example of married people in your life.

I want you to win! But to do so, you need to develop real relationships with some people who are already winning.

Investor vs. Invested.

Now I know what you're thinking. What am I supposed to do? Get rid of all my friends? Are there some friends in your life that have too much of a voice? You don't want to give anybody control over your life. I love and believe in people and their comebacks. Therefore, I'm not promoting the idea of just leaving them high and dry.

But here's a tip to help you position your relationships in a way that's going to be the best for you and them: Determine whether you're the investor or invested.

Most relationships have someone who's the investor.

They're the ones who might be a little bit further along in their journey. They have the life experience to share with those they live with.

On the flip side, investors choose to invest in somebody. That's who I like to call the invested. If you're the invested, you're on the receiving end. You get the benefit of wisdom from the investor.

Investors shape the lives of others while the invested get their lives shaped. It's fine to be in either position, as long as you understand what your role is.

There's people from my past who I used to be really good friends with. I run into them from time to time. Want to know what I do when I see them? I shake their hand, show them some love, and ask how I can pray for them. I don't allow their life to shape mine, I instead want to shape theirs.

And when you find someone who has the wisdom and life experience to be an investor, be humble enough to identify it. Reach out to them first for advice. Ask the right questions. Absorb and act on what they say! They're in your life for a reason. Be thankful and take full advantage of it.

Comeback Challenge.

The comeback challenge I'm going to give you this chapter has two parts to it. Let's break down part one.

First, spend some time evaluating your circle.

If you never slow down to evaluate the contents of your live, you'll never actually change. What voices are speaking into your life? Are they leading you in the direction of the destination you'd ultimately like to end up?

If the answer is no, you might need to re-define that relationship. You might need to become an investor to them and find a new investor for you. Depending on where you're at mentally, you may even need to cut that relationship off. Voices that aren't building your future need to be replaced.

Second, find a mentor.

Who's someone you admire? It doesn't have to be somebody who is a multi-millionaire or has written ten books on success. Who's a step further than where you are? They have something of infinite value to offer you.

Maybe it's your boss. You may not love everything they do, but they did something to become a boss. They became a leader for a reason.

Having a mentor takes humility. It takes admittance that someone else has something to teach you. That means you have to be willing to own the fact that you don't know everything!

Once you identify who you want your mentor to be, reach out and ask them! We sometimes listen to the voices of fear or insecurity in our heads, telling us they're too busy or wouldn't be interested. But the worst thing that can happen is they say no. And if they do, that means they weren't supposed to be your mentor. But it also means someone else out there is.

Your comeback won't happen alone, but only when you open up your life to others. Change is available. We can get there *together*.

Bonus Challenge.

I know looking for a mentor can be extremely intimidating. I created a blueprint that I still use to this day when approaching a mentor. If you want to use that blueprint also, check it out at **youllneverchange.com/mentor**.

Eleven.

THEY SAID I'LL NEVER
MAKE A COMEBACK

"HATE IT OR LOVE IT, THE UNDERDOG'S ON TOP"
[50 CENT]

I gained confidence as some things slowly started to fall into place. I took the steps of kicking addiction, becoming a reliable employee, and finding a mentor. And with each step I took in the right direction, my motivation continued to grow.

Let me be clear. Overcoming addiction was one of the hardest things I've ever done. But it wasn't the goal of my life, it was the side effect of wanting and chasing more. The purpose of this book isn't to teach you the fundamentals of overcoming addiction. There's plenty of 12 step programs that can do that. This book is meant to teach you how to create the life you've always wanted.

Eventually, I found myself wanting to face what I had previously been terrified of; the people I screwed over. I wanted to reach out to those I had cheated, stolen from, and treated poorly. Bad decisions always have consequences. I had to face them, but unfortunately, some people in my life did as well. And while I deserved all of the repercussions that came my way, they did not. And I genuinely felt awful about that.

In recovery circles, there's a concept called "making amends." It's a fancy way of saying, "righting your wrongs." I did everything I could, even though it wasn't always much, to try to fix what old Nate destroyed.

The first person I reached out to was a lady who let me borrow her car when mine had broken down. When I was still running around, I drove to Pittsburgh and Cleveland casinos on an alarmingly frequent basis. The quickest and best way to get there was on the toll roads. As you can imagine, the old Nate wasn't crazy about paying to drive on a highway, so I decided not to. Instead of stopping to pay the toll to an attendant, I went through the EZ Pass Lane, even though I didn't have an EZ Pass. Cameras snapped pictures of the license plate and mailed it to the owner.

Long story short, this poor lady helped me out by letting me borrow her car, and I repaid her by making her pay all of the tickets I accumulated. At the time, I planned on never talking to her again. So when I decided to make the call, I was pretty terrified.

I'm sure it was entertaining listening to my nervous, shaky voice trying on the other side of the line. It went something like this:

"Hello?" She answered suspiciously, seeing the name "Nate Dukes" pop up on her phone for the first time in a long time. I responded on a bit of a delay. "Hey! It's um, Nate. I've got to be honest with you, I don't really know the right way to go about this, but this is me putting myself out there. I'm trying to change. I don't want to be the old me anymore. I know I really screwed you over with those tickets when you let me borrow your car. I want to ask for your forgiveness and help make it right in any way that I can."

My thoughts were jumbled as I rambled on for a while. It definitely wasn't the smoothest apology ever, but it felt good to face my past as a new me. I was proud of myself for calling.

Honestly, she wasn't super receptive at first. To put it a little bit more realistically, she kind of tore me a new one. It made sense. I wounded her and then opened up that wound. Hurt is what she responded with, and understandably so. I chose not to get hurt by her hurt. Your emotions will try to trick you into doing that. But I was determined beforehand I would take full ownership of my mistake. I asked her how much she ended up paying for the tickets, and assured her I was sending a check for that amount as soon as we hung up the phone. (I had to cut a lot of grass to cut that check)

Then something really cool happened. She forgave me. She even encouraged me and wished me luck for the future. It felt really good! It's powerful when someone affirms the changes you're making and the direction you're heading.

Next, I hit up a buddy of mine who had always been a better friend to me than I had been to him. He had invited me to his wedding when I was in the middle of my addiction, which was a huge day for him, and I no-call no-showed him. When I called him and took ownership for being inconsiderate, he met me with understanding and forgiveness. It was the first step in rebuilding our relationship.

But I need to share something essential with you. It didn't always go like that. Not everybody who I asked to forgive me actually did. Some people stayed angry and expressed it through some pretty colorful and memorable language. Others had no interest in even talking to me.

Maybe the most challenging call I made was to my old business partner. Considering I stole a large sum of money and almost bankrupt the beautiful business we built together, this was the big one. I reached out multiple times in an attempt to start the process of fixing some of the damage I caused. He wanted nothing to do with it or me. Even to this day, we still haven't spoken. If he ever reads this book, I want him to know that I'm sorry and still want to go on a journey of restoration. But if he doesn't want that, I also respect him for it.

It sucks that I haven't been able to fix that relationship. He wasn't just my business partner; he was one of my best friends. I not only feel terrible for screwing over my friend, but I also miss him in my life. However, I've learned a few valuable lessons through his rejection.

Not everybody is going to forgive you, and that's okay. You might have hurt somebody so badly that they're not emotionally capable of letting you back in their lives. It would stir up too much pain. But the fear of un-forgiveness should never keep you from seeking forgiveness. The misconception of forgiveness is that it's only for the person you wronged. And it is for them. But equally important, it's for you. Every time you say you're sorry, you free yourself from guilt and shame.

The right thing to do was to try to make it right. I would have hated living my entire life knowing I royally messed up that friendship and done absolutely nothing about it. Now, at least I know I tried to do the right thing. And at the end of the day, I take peace in that. Because it's all I have the power to do.

The fear of un-forgiveness should never keep you from seeking forgiveness.

You're responsible for doing the right thing, not for how people respond to it.

We can't control the responses of others. I guess life would be a lot easier if we could. But they are their own people, who have the freedom to respond to us in whichever way they decide best. When it comes to restoration, we can't clean up their side of the street, but we can always take care of ours.

Now that you're trying to move forward with your comeback, you have to be willing to put yourself out there. You can't allow the fear of somebody's response, perception, or opinion to keep you from doing what is right- for yourself and those around you.

You're responsible for doing the right thing, not for how people respond to it.

Your comeback will stir up all sorts of mixed responses. Some will support you; others will want nothing to do with you. Some will want to run with you; others will want to run away from you. Some will encourage you; others will cuss you out.

Your change is not contingent upon their response. You can't change their belief in you. But you can continue to change yourself regardless of what they have to say about it. Responses can only knock you off course if you allow them to.

Attracting Haters.

The unfortunate truth is that you'll always have people in your life who don't understand, believe, or support you any time you try to change. For me, I put a label on these types of people so I can easily identify them and quickly keep them from distracting or discouraging me. I like to call them haters. Let's spell out a clear definition, so we're working from the same frame of reference as we talk about haters for the rest of this chapter.

Hater (hātér): anyone who doesn't support who you're becoming because of who you've been

Sometimes people become haters intentionally, yet other times it's unintentional. Sometimes hate comes from afar, while other times it's those closest to you. Haters can be past friends, present friends, those you admire, social media followers, or family members. Regardless of the source, opposition is inevitable.

Haters develop for different reasons, but here's some of the most common I've experienced:

Change is inward before its outward. My buddy from the bar didn't want anything to do with me because he knew the old me. So when I reached out, I knew I wasn't the old me anymore, but he had no idea! Sure, I could say I'm trying to change. But anybody can say just about anything. Change starts as inspiration but is only proven by action. I hadn't proven I was a new Nate, yet. Therefore, he thought he'd be opening himself back up to the old Nate, who was capable of lying, stealing, and hurting him all over again.

People who have been hurt by the old you may have a hard time wrapping their minds around a new you. It doesn't take away from the internal changes you've been making. That's where change must grow, develop, and mature! But as long as it's internal, it's invisible to everyone but you. Therefore, you'll always be battling against the reputation you built with people from your past. They may not believe in who you're becoming, because they still only know who you've been.

People project their crap on you. People with issues inevitably project those issues on those around them. If you're reading this book, you know this to be true because your past has painfully affected the people around you. Hurt people hurt other people. That's the way it goes.

When others actually see you start to change, it stirs up all sorts of emotions in them. Unfortunately, most human beings are continually comparing themselves to people around them to measure how they're doing. It's unhealthy, but it happens.

When you start to move toward success, it might stir up insecurity in those who feel unsuccessful. As you begin taking risks, it will most likely bring fear to the surface of the lives of those around you. Sometimes they push back because they're trying to protect you from failure. Other times, they're trying to keep you down so they can continue to feel good about themselves. People's issues with themselves often times come disguised as an issue with you.

People are crazy. Honestly, sometimes there's no other

explanation. There's usually a reason behind why people hate on you, but it's not always obvious. They might be bored, bitter, or just flat out mean. Think about how crazy the internet is for a second. Have you ever looked at the comment section of a YouTube video with more than one million views? They are usually filled with hate. You know these online haters as "keyboard commandos" who throw shade apparently for no other reason but to be seen.

Whatever you put out into the world inevitably attracts people. I like to think of it like preparing food for a party. You put hours of hard work into the appetizers, dinner, and desserts for the friends you invited over. They look and taste unbelievable when you lay them out across the counter to be served buffet-style. While your friends get to enjoy the beautiful food you worked incredibly hard on, it also attracts flies as it sits on the counter. In the same way, whenever you start to put something really extraordinary out into the world, it impacts the people you're called to but it also attracts the crazy ones.

Long story short, people hate for all sorts of different reasons, but there is one common thread I typically see. It's the biggest lesson I've learned about haters, and if you can understand this, the haters in your life won't hold nearly as much weight.

Haters are a sign of significance.

Our minds naturally associate haters with negativity. We think we must be doing something wrong because people don't like it or us. But actually, the opposite is true.

Becoming a better person than you currently are is hard. Therefore, not everyone is going to believe you can. But the fact that it's hard, and even seemingly impossible in the eyes of some, means it's worth going after.

If your change starts to bring out the insecurity and fears in others, that means you're becoming someone who they could not. It's a sign that you're dreaming big, and even more importantly, headed in the right direction.

Are crazy people annoying? Sure. But they wouldn't even be paying attention to you if you weren't doing something, while they're at home doing nothing.

I wouldn't be overly concerned about the presence of haters in your life. In fact, I'd be more concerned if you never experience any opposition. Haters follow movement. Therefore, if you have none, a fair question to ask yourself is, "am I moving in a way that matters?"

Handling Haters

If haters gonna hate, we have to come up with a strategy of how to handle it. We all know how powerful encouragement and support can be. They build you up in the right direction. Unfortunately, hate can be just as impactful. But rather than building you up, it tears you down. What should we do in the face of opposition? Here are a few thoughts:

Learn to coach yourself. A good coach's role is to push you past obstacles and pull out the greatness inside of you. Often times, when we receive hate, especially from multiple sources, it feels like nobody is in our corner. It's in those moments that we must choose to become our own coach.

It's crucial to grab ahold of something bigger than yourself so that when things get tough, you can motivate yourself to keep moving forward. For me, it was my spirituality. When people didn't believe in who I was becoming, I held on to the confidence that God did. Therefore, I could encourage myself to continue moving in that direction. Whoever you're trying to become, hold on to it. And when other voices try to lead you in different directions, make sure yours stays true to what you want deep on the inside of you.

Limit voices that try to limit you. It's easy to make the negative voice the loudest voice in your life. For some reason, we tend to brush off encouragement and hold onto hate and criticism. Try to flip that the other way around in your life.

Whenever someone says something discouraging to you, remember it's just one opinion. And opinions aren't facts. Learn to recognize voices of hate for what they are, process them as opinions, and leave them where they belong- in the past!

Use negative feedback as fuel. Feedback is one of the greatest tools we have in life. It's invaluable when people who genuinely want what's best for us are honest with us. They can help us see blind spots, improve in areas of weakness, and provide game-changing perspective. Healthy feedback, when accepted, is a greenhouse to our growth.

However, feedback from a hater isn't usually healthy. While there may be some things you can learn, I wouldn't make a habit of taking feedback from people who have mixed motivations. If you sense someone has the goal of building you up, listen, and apply what's useful. But if it seems someone simply wants to tear you down, don't allow it to shake your confidence.

However, even if the feedback is negative, it doesn't mean it's completely useless. You can use it as fuel. I titled this book "You'll Never Change" because I got told that a lot. My guess is that maybe you have, as well. And if you haven't heard it yet, it's probably only a matter of time.

Haters can serve as a source of motivation. You can change. You can prove them wrong. You can become the person you were always created to be. You can do the things they said you'd never be able to do. And you don't have to rub it in their faces either. Ultimate gratification is to prove them wrong and be the bigger person.

Haters aren't a sign that you can't change; they mean that you already are! As long as we respond in the right way, we'll continue to head in the right direction.

Comeback Challenge.

If you're serious about your comeback, you're going to experience some haters along the way. Trust me, if not yet, you will! But the voices that want to derail you can actually propel you. I want to make sure that happens. So here's your comeback challenge for this chapter: **Learn to look in the mirror and coach yourself.**

Every negative voice needs a positive one to overcome it. And I can't promise you that you'll always have access to positivity when you need it. Unless, of course, you learn to be that voice.

The way you need to coach yourself varies depending on what direction you're headed and what season you're in. I know it might feel weird, but get in the habit of complimenting, encouraging, and pushing yourself! Here are some coaching phrases that might get the wheels of your brain turning:

"Just because they can't see it, doesn't mean it isn't happening."
"You're doing better than you think."
"Nobody can tell you who you're going to be."
"Who you were is not who you are."

Your comeback requires coaching! From others, but also from yourself. You'd be amazed at how far you can coach yourself to go.

Bonus Challenge.

Making amends with someone you've hurt can be incredibly difficult but incredibly rewarding. The good news is it doesn't always have to be monetary, especially if you're broke right now. I've created a list of different ways you can make amends to help you get started. This can be a very powerful tool on your comeback journey. Check it out at **youllneverchange. com/amend**s.

Twelve.

HOW CAN I TRUST MYSELF?

"I DON'T NEED TO LIE NO MORE. NOWADAYS ALL I DO IS SHINE, TAKE A BREATH AND EASE MY MIND."
[MAC MILLER]

I had a rather significant realization as I journeyed down the road to my comeback. My inspiration wasn't leading to all that much action. Sure, I had become a more respectable member of society who no longer stole cars from people's driveways. I moved past the likelihood of prison becoming a possibility. But I knew there was more to my life than "staying out of trouble." Existence wasn't enough anymore. I wanted to contribute to and make a mark on the world.

But I had a problem. I had no clue how to live out what I pictured in my imagination. I knew how to dream dreams, but I didn't know how to do dreams. It left me living in the tension of frustration. It even sounds frustrating doesn't it? I had a fear of my behavior changing, but my impact not mattering. I knew I needed to do something.

I kept most of this inside, but my mentor could see it in me. At the end of one of our sessions, he suggested that I go through Rust City College, a two-year leadership academy associated with the church I was going to. It was the same school he attended and therefore he was a pretty big believer in it. He didn't ask for an answer right away but encouraged me to think and pray about it.

I mustered up my best fake smile and assured him I would as I walked away from our session. But truthfully, I had no plans whatsoever to pray about it, and I had already thought about it in as much detail as needed. The answer was a big, fat, "no thank you."

During our session the next week, I let Brad know he had the wrong guy and I came prepared with my list of reasons. I felt I'd made too many mistakes and hurt too many people.

It's almost as if he didn't hear my answer. In fact, I don't even really remember him responding. Good mentors are persistent like that. He never pressured me, but he continued to find creative ways to keep Rust City College at the forefront of my mind. Whenever he'd sense complacency, frustration, or boredom from me, he'd dangle the idea of the school in front of me. Between him and God not letting me forget about it, I eventually caved. My big, fat, "no thank you" turned into an intimidated, "let's give it a shot."

My commitment to the school was sparked by me getting really honest with myself. I had dreams of what I wanted to do in life but wasn't actually moving toward any of them. The root of the problem was a lack of confidence. I didn't know how to move toward them and never investigated because I didn't believe in myself. There was a deficiency in me when it came to the education and skillsets needed to achieve.

On top of my insecurity, I was also prideful. Not a great combination. It's easier to hide behind "being too good" for something than admitting you're afraid of it. And that's one of the biggest reasons I didn't want to go to school at first. I was twenty-nine years old and felt like I should already be established in a career. Even further than that, I had already owned a business and tasted success. When most others my age were starting to thrive, I felt like going to school was going in the wrong direction.

Rust City College was one of the most humbling steps I'd ever taken in my life. It was also one of the most defining. I had to drop my ego, accept that I didn't know everything, and become teachable. What felt like a step backward ended up propelling me forward in ways I would never have imagined. I ended up developing as a leader, meeting my wife, and becoming a staff member at Rust City Church, afterward. Those are some of the most significant things that have happened in my entire life! But they only happened because of one reason. I made a commitment and kept it.

As always, I'll be honest with you. It wasn't always easy to follow through with that commitment over those two years. When it came to this program, you only got out as much as you put in. And it demanded you to give a lot of yourself. But because I knew where I wanted to go, I gave myself to it time and time again. I stayed up late studying, showed up at community outreaches with a positive attitude when I didn't feel like it, and stepped into leadership opportunities when I was afraid. And all of it stretched me. Are you doing things that stretch you?

Those two years were filled with me entering one challenging position after another. I lived in a never-ending state of being squeezed. Although being squeezed doesn't feel good, it does force you to look at what's inside of you. There were moments when I wasn't crazy about who I was under pressure. But every single time, the people around me helped me grow. They were relentless about not allowing me to slip underneath the standard of who I was called to be.

It's said that diamonds are only created under pressure. And I was under a lot of pressure. Not to perform, but rather to develop. Dreams only happen through development. And time and time again, I had to choose to keep my commitment to development rather than throw in the towel.

As a freshman student, qualities like frustration and impatience came out of me when things got hard. By the end of the two years, the squeezing forced out the character, leadership, and gifts developed on the inside of me.

Although being squeezed doesn't feel good, it does force you to look at what's inside of you.

Making a commitment isn't hard. Keeping one is. What you choose to do when things get challenging matters. Exit doors will open themselves up along the journey. And typically, they're super tempting. But the comfort of giving up won't pull out the character necessary for your calling. Only commitment to the process can do that.

Talking vs. Walking

I like to look at commitment through the lens of promise. From the time we were kids, we've grown accustomed to making promises. During adolescence, most are innocent enough. Maybe we promised our parents to finish our green beans or clean our rooms before friends came over. But as we become adults, the weight attached to our promises increases. Promises to stay faithful to a spouse, raise kids right, or meet a deadline all have significant rewards and repercussions attached to them.

Whether we realize it or not, we also make promises to ourselves all the time. Sometimes they disguise themselves as motivated thoughts or seasonal goals. Regardless, self-promises have implications as well. When we fulfill the promises we make to ourselves, we experience the positive reward that comes our way. But when we fail to keep them, we experience negative repercussions as well.

Some not-so-great effects may be as simple as continuing to carry around the extra twenty pounds or not being able to kick smoking. Do those repercussions suck? Absolutely. But I believe one negative side effect serves to be the most detrimental every time you break a promise to yourself. That side effect is a loss of trust in yourself.

Trust in any relationship is a huge deal. We might not think this way, but it's also really important to trust our relationship with ourselves. When we follow through on our self-promises, we honor ourselves by doing what we said we would. But every time we don't follow through, we break self-trust little by little. We prove to ourselves that we don't do what we say. And when you don't follow through enough times, eventually, you'll stop making commitments. Uncommitted people become complacent people. And those who are complacent don't follow through with their comeback story.

I learned a lot during my time as a student at Rust City College. I learned how to foster a relationship with God, lead groups of different sizes, inspire people, and communicate effectively. But the most important thing I learned was this:

Self-confidence is created by keeping promises to yourself.

Most people are good at talking the talk, but very few are good at walking the walk. Why is that? Because talking is easy! It doesn't cost you anything. Walking, on the other hand, definitely does. Most of us would have no problem talking to a friend for three hours. But it's a lot more difficult walking around a track for the same period of time.

What things have you been talking to yourself about?

"I need to start going to the gym more."
"I'm going to stop smoking weed soon."
"I'd like to work on my relationship with my parents."
"I'd love to go back to school."
"I'm going to become a better person."
"One of these days, I'm going to write that book."

Can I coach you for a second? You owe it to yourself to stop talking and start walking. Every time you make a promise to yourself and don't keep it, you're becoming a little less confident in yourself. Let today be the day you become credible again. Decide what self-promises are worthy of making and fight to walk them out every day.

Process

One of the reasons it's difficult to walk out promises we make to ourselves is the process. Honestly, I hate that word! Most driven people do. We like to see results as soon as a dream pops into our heads. It'd be great if we could see the end after one day of effort. But that's just not the way life works.

I didn't want to attend Rust City College for two years because of fear of the process. Since I had already built a business before, I tried to expedite myself to the same pinnacle of success I had already reached. But it wasn't that simple. This time, I needed to succeed at becoming a better person while accomplishing my goals. Different contexts require different processes.

I've found those that seem to win the most are never too entitled for the process. Leaders who aren't afraid to start small, get dirty, and figure it out are the best kind. They inevitably experience failure along the way, as nobody can entirely avoid that. But if you were to examine their lives, it almost seems as if excellence follows them. It's not because they have a magic touch or get extremely lucky. Most of the time, it doesn't even come down to skill or talent. Rather, it boils down to navigating the process well.

All promises require processes. We'd prefer that results were microwaved. But they taste a lot better when they're slow-cooked. Before you make a promise to yourself, do so with the understanding there will be a long, grueling, messy process attached to it.

If you promise yourself to lift five days a week, you'll have to fight through days you don't feel like it.

If you promise yourself to get a degree, there will be nights of extreme stress and no sleep.

If you promise yourself to kick your bad habits, temptation that feels irresistible will continue to knock on your door.

If you promise yourself to start a business, you'll have to pick yourself up over-and-over again when you feel like a complete failure.

We tend to admire the finished product. But behind every product is a process you know nothing about. Only the person who went through it understands the depths of it. And because we didn't experience the process, we buy into the myth that maybe we can skip it.

The dreams that live deep within our hearts require stewarding a small start. We get it backward. We think that once we get something big, we'll take excellent care of it. Big looks different for all of us. It could be a big job, big opportunity, or

Success is not a reward it's a responsibility.

the big responsibility of being a parent. But the truth is, we'll never have big unless we handle small, first. Success is not a reward it's a responsibility.

One of my favorite leadership lessons on stewardship is found as a story in the Bible. I know that not all of you reading believe in God, but even if you're not a believer this will still help you.

In Matthew 25:14-29 there's three workers who are each given bags of silver from their boss. The two who were given the highest number of bags invested the money and earned more. But the one who was given only one bag did nothing with it.

The boss rewarded the two workers who worked hard by giving them more. But he took everything away from the one who did nothing. In other words, the ones who handled the small well were given more. But the boss knew he couldn't trust the worker who didn't do a good job with the little responsibility he was given.

The dreams we have for our lives work the same way. We can't wait for success to become good stewards. Significant things only start to develop in our lives when we handle the process attached to the promises we make ourselves. So yes, your job at McDonalds matters right now.

The things in front of you might seem small. Can I encourage you for a second? It's not about the size of your opportunity, it's about how you steward your opportunity. Handle it well—all of it. If you do so for long enough, you'll be amazed at the opportunities that will come your way.

Comeback Challenge.

Your comeback challenge for this chapter is simple but will take effort: **Make a promise to yourself and keep it.**

Here's my encouragement. If you haven't been able to count on yourself as of late, don't start with anything crazy. Pick something that's attainable, but still challenges you a little bit. Once you decide what the self-promise is, write it down somewhere. Make it official. But most importantly, do it.

Maybe you want to start by journaling, preparing a healthy meal every night for dinner, listening to one podcast a day, or scheduling an appointment with a counselor.

Whatever it looks like for you, make the promise, keep it, and develop the confidence your comeback will require.

Bonus Challenge.

If you haven't figured this out already I'm a fan of hearing about your progress. In this chapter we talked about self confidence, going through a process, and keeping promises. Send me an update of your story at **youllneverchange.com/ story**. I'd love to share it.

You can go to **@whoisnatedukes** on instagram to see other people's comeback stories.

Thirteen.

PROVE THEM WRONG

"ALLOW ME TO RE-INTRODUCE MYSELF"
[JAY-Z]

The time between my release from jail and graduation from Rust City College felt like a grind. I could feel myself changing as a person but wasn't necessarily living the life I had envisioned. The internal me had undergone a pretty extreme overhaul. Meanwhile, I was making progress externally but was nowhere near a finished product.

That's how change happens most of the time. A lot of work produces results little by little. Until one day you look back and everything seems to have shifted.

In the months following Rust City College, everything seemed to shift. The years of hard work on myself started to become visible to everyone else. The vision I shaped my goals around finally started to become a reality!

Where my life stands now is drastically different from where it was. The Nate I am now is nothing like the Nate I described at the beginning of this book.

A lot of work produces results little by little.

I started dating my future wife, Jenna, during my two years at college. Luckily for me, we got married shortly after graduation. I know this is a cliche thing to say, but she's one-hundred percent the best thing that has ever happened to me. That statement may be over-used, but I say it because it's true. She loves me unconditionally despite my past and present imperfections. She believes in me, pushes me forward, and holds me accountable. And she has just the right amount of loving-sassiness (a whole lot) to keep me in check.

I went from stealing cars to now owning two of them. I guess the truth is that I own one, and Jenna owns the other. But the beautiful thing about marriage is what's hers is now mine. Looking back, it's so crazy to me that at my lowest, I had to steal a vehicle just to get around. It seems small, but I don't take it for granted.

Jenna and I bought a duplex together. We live on one side and rent out the other. My desire to make money used to be driven by greed and my gambling addiction. It also was empty. I had no plan in place for how to generate more income or manage it well. Now, my financial strategy is driven by the responsibility to provide for my family. And we actually have tangible assets, like our duplex, that help us build wealth through passive income.

My career path is one I would never have anticipated. The jump to ministry is not one most bar-owners ever make. The old me didn't care how my business affected people's lives, as long as I made money. Our biggest customers were those who had addiction problems or were trying to drink their hardships away. I went from enabling people to break their lives to empowering people to build them.

The truth is, my present wouldn't have been possible without God's grace. He brought the right people into my life at the right time, gave me strength when I needed it the most, and inspired me to love people by the way He loved me. I'm unbelievably grateful for the life He's given to me!

Trust me, I'm not trying to brag on myself. Instead, I'm trying to make a point.

If I can do it, you can do it.

I've made some of the worst decisions you can make. The lows I've experienced are more drastic than most. And the lack of belief I had in myself felt like it hit some record lows.

But I changed. You might be looking at my life, saying, "it isn't the one I want." I totally understand. We have different dreams, goals, and visions. We were designed and wired to be uniquely different.

You may want a different life than me, but the way of getting there is the same. Principles produce. The principles in this book guided me into my comeback. If you choose to apply them to your life, they'll guide you into yours as well.

Comeback Equation.

I'm not a big school guy, but if I could pick my favorite subject now, it'd be algebra. I know, I know. Some of you hate algebra. Others don't remember how to do it. But hang with me for a second! This is going to be the most straightforward math teaching you've ever experienced.

Algebra is full of equations. When it boils down to it, equations are cause and effect. When you add two numbers together, you get a sum. When you multiply two numbers, you get a product. I'm drawn to the certainty of it all. Taking the right steps in front of the equal sign guarantees you'll get the right ones on back end.

I've created an equation for a comeback that I want to share with you. I believe if you apply it to your life, you'll experience the comeback you've been in search of. Why?

When you do the right things, you get the right results

The biggest lesson I've learned through this entire journey is pretty simple. When you do the right things, you get the right results. This formula will equate to your comeback and real life-change.

Vision + Decisions x Time = Your Comeback

Vision plus decisions multiplied by time equals your comeback. For those of you who still struggle with math like me, let me break down what this means

Our talk about vision was all the way back in chapter three, so here's a little refresher. The starting place of vision is playing for tomorrow instead of today. To develop a vision, we must slow down and ask ourselves where we want our lives to go and who we actually want to be. For vision to matter, we must give ourselves permission to dream again. It has nothing to do with where we currently are. It has everything to do with where we're headed in the future.

Decisions have been a common theme throughout this book. Decisions are what determine our direction. If you make bad ones, your life starts moving in a bad direction. But when you make good ones, you inevitably move in a good one. The best decisions are ones filtered through wisdom and some people in your life who have been where you want to go. When we make decisions that line up with our vision, our journey becomes exciting and rewarding.

While vision and decisions can be challenging, time is the hardest part of this equation. It's easy to have a vision and make good decisions for a few days, but can you maintain it for a few years? We tend to overestimate how much we can accomplish in a short period but underestimate how much we can accomplish in a long period. Vision and decisions are multiplied by time in the comeback equation because multiplication produces a larger number than addition. And real results take a really large amount of time. If you're going to reach them, you must not only have the patience for the process, but also continue to do what's right even when you're bored and tired. The greatest comeback stories weren't made after a moment but years.

At the risk of making your comeback sound overly simplified, this formula works. It'll require extreme amounts of determination, dedication, and discipline to get there. But you can get there!

Develop a vision. Who do you want to be? Maybe a nicer person, better spouse, or someone who's at peace with yourself. What do you want to do? Possibly you wish to become a coach, businessman, or addiction counselor.

Make the right decisions. What's going to get you there? You might need to go to counseling, spend more time in the gym, meditate, read a few books, go back to school, or take some significant steps of faith.

Give it time. Wake up and do the right things day after day. Do them when you're inspired and when you're not.

Choose to work at them even when it feels like they aren't working.

Your comeback doesn't take talent. It takes your willingness to grind at the right things until you get the right results.

Comeback Challenge

Every chapter in this book so far has had a "comeback challenge." Most of them have been practical action steps that you can take right now. I hope you've been doing them. I also hope they've started the process of changing your life. If you've been skipping out, go back after this chapter and begin to apply these challenges every day.

For the last challenge, I'm going to switch it up on you a little bit. I'm not going to give you something practical to do, but rather an idea to believe. Here's your comeback challenge: **Believe you can change.**

I titled this book "You'll Never Change" because so many people think it's true. But I want to let you know something that possibly nobody else has told you in awhile. I BELIEVE IN YOU. I'm begging you, please don't skim over that. Take a second and let that sink in. Someone really does believe in you.

However, my hope is that you don't stop at me believing in you. I need you to believe in you. Because once you believe in yourself, you'll start to operate differently. We have an amazing ability as human beings to become what we believe.

When I was in some of the lowest places in my life, I wouldn't have believed someone if they told me someday I'd be married and living out my dreams. I would have written them off as being crazy.

I remember lying in bed even before my arrest, feeling

the weight of my present reality settle heavily on my shoulders. Even though my body was relaxed, my mind was far from it. The truth that nobody even liked me because of who I'd become felt like it weighed thousands of pounds.

Now my life is full of love. I live in complete awareness of how much God, and the people who matter the most in my life, love me. I've also given my life to loving others.

When I picked up my felony, I thought my future was over. But if you're reading this book, it means I'm an author. I didn't even know that felons were allowed to write books!

What happened? I debunked the myth that said, "you'll never change," and I fought like hell for my comeback.

Do me a favor and put your hand on your chest for a few seconds. Was there a heartbeat? If you're still reading, I'm assuming there was. That means you're still alive. And as long as you're alive, your story is still being written.

Regardless of your past, you have the opportunity to become the hero of your future. It's not up to other people, your lack of education, or crappy situation.

It's up to you.

You can change. Go create your comeback and prove them wrong.

Bonus Challenge.

Fulfillment doesn't come from helping yourself, it comes from helping other people. Share this book with someone who needs to make a comeback the same way you do.

Notes.

CHAPTER 2

1. "Vision." Merriam-Webster, Merriam-Webster, www.merriam-webster.com/dictionary/vision.

CHAPTER 4

1. Mineo, Liz. "Good Genes Are Nice, Buy Joy Is Better." Harvard Gazette, Harvard Gazette, 11 Apr. 2017, news.harvard.edu/gazette/story/2017/04/over-nearly-80-years-harvard-study-has-been-showing-how-to-live-a-healthy-and-happy-life/.

CHAPTER 7

1. "Amazing Grace." Wikipedia, Wikimedia Foundation, 25 Sept. 2020, en.wikipedia.org/wiki/Amazing_Grace.

CHAPTER 9

1. "Floyd Mayweather Jr. vs. Conor McGregor." Wikipedia, Wikimedia Foundation, 6 Oct. 2020, en.wikipedia.org/wiki/Floyd_Mayweather_Jr._vs._Conor_McGregor.

CHAPTER 12

1. Holy Bible, New Living Translation. Tyndale House Foundation, 2015.

MAKE SURE
TO REVIEW THIS
BOOK ON

amazon

Made in the USA
Middletown, DE
14 July 2021

44152935R00084